The Complete Rosary

OTHER LOYOLA PRESS BOOKS
BY WILLIAM G. STOREY

A Prayer Book of Catholic Devotions
Praying the Seasons and Feasts of the Church Year

Novenas
Prayers of Intercession and Devotion

the
Complete
Rosary

A Guide to
Praying the
Mysteries

William G. Storey

LoyolaPress.

Chicago

LOYOLAPRESS.
3441 N. ASHLAND AVENUE
CHICAGO, ILLINOIS 60657
(800) 621-1008
WWW.LOYOLABOOKS.ORG

Nihil Obstat
Reverend Louis J. Cameli, S.T.D.
Censor Deputatus
October 19, 2005

Imprimatur
Reverend George J. Rassas
Vicar General
Archdiocese of Chicago
October 21, 2005

The *Nihil Obstat* and *Imprimatur* are official declarations that a book is free of doctrinal and moral error. No implication is contained therein that those who have granted the *Nihil Obstat* and *Imprimatur* agree with the content, opinions, or statements expressed. Nor do they assume any legal responsibility associated with publication.

Cover and interior design by Megan Duffy Rostan

Library of Congress Cataloging-in-Publication Data
Storey, William George, 1923–
    The complete rosary : a guide to praying the mysteries / William
G. Storey.
        p. cm.
    Includes bibliographical references.
    ISBN 0-8294-2351-6
    1. Rosary. 2. Mysteries of the Rosary. 3. Mary, Blessed Virgin,
Saint—Devotion to   I. Title.
    BX2163.S76 2006
    242'.74—dc22

                                                    2005026798

Printed in the United States of America
06 07 08 09 10 Versa 10 9 8 7 6 5 4 3 2

To the great Mother of God, Mary most holy,
Help of Christians, Refuge of sinners,
Health of the sick.

CONTENTS

Introduction

I was born and raised in a religiously divided family. Most of my relatives were fallen-away Methodists like my father and some of my aunts, or Anglicans like my grandfathers, great-grandfather, and my mother. A few were Roman Catholics like my maternal grandmother, Florence Agnes Valois, a French Canadian. Of all my relatives, she had the greatest religious influence on my young life.

During my childhood and teenage years I was an Anglican and attended church regularly—Matins, Holy Eucharist, Evensong—every Sunday but never caught even a whiff of Marian devotion. In paging through the Book of Common Prayer I discovered some few surviving medieval feasts dedicated to

Mary, but since they were never mentioned, much less celebrated, they meant nothing to me. Grandma Valois, however, old and sickly as she was, still recited her prayers in French and had a bedroom festooned with holy pictures, holy water, and rosaries. She also received a Catholic magazine dedicated to Our Lady of Victory, and in it I found enough mention of the Rosary devotion to give me a kind of skeleton outline of its contents—Mysteries, Our Fathers, Hail Marys (Ave Marias), Glorias—but nary a mention of its purpose or its spiritual point.

Attracted by the doctrine and practice of the real presence of Jesus in the Blessed Sacrament and the teaching of the Quebec Catechism, at eighteen I became a Roman Catholic. This move brought me into full contact with the Roman liturgy (old style), parish missions by the Redemptorist Fathers, the Way of the Cross, retreats, vigil lights, scapulars, novenas, and, strangest of all, the Rosary, recited in families and in church. Several devout Catholic families were very kind to me, and when I visited their homes I was introduced to the family Rosary: five decades after dinner on our knees on a linoleum or wood floor, recited fairly quickly, with a bare mention of a mystery before each decade. It was often followed by the Litany of Loreto and another string of Our Fathers and Hail Marys for "special intentions." For me it was a paralyzing rather than an edifying experience. I was impressed by the regularity of the practice in such families but found it too repetitive and puzzling and very hard on the knees.

Fortunately, my pastor gave me a Latin/English copy of the Little Office of the Blessed Virgin Mary for daily use, and I found its hymns, psalms, readings, and prayers far more attractive and formative than the Rosary. I soon discovered, however, that my pastor, our parish nuns, and I were the only people who even knew about the Little Office, much less prayed it. Nevertheless, my pastor did not attempt to give me any instruction on *how* to pray either the Little Office or the Rosary.

My most difficult experience of the Rosary was praying it in church on Sunday evenings. Reciting five decades at a pretty fast clip on a bare wood kneeler was even less edifying to me than reciting them on a kitchen floor. For me, the best part of that evening service was Benediction of the Blessed Sacrament: the visible host in a golden monstrance, hymns, incense, and the blessing itself—well worth waiting for!

A bit later I experienced sung Vespers in a first-rate cathedral; but even Vespers was preceded by a quick recitation of the Rosary. For all too long the Rosary remained a conundrum to me. I just could not discover its point!

Even more mystifying was the emphasis laid on the Rosary in pious literature. Apparently Our Lady wanted it said for world peace and for the conversion of Russia. My question was why in the world Mary would recommend such an uninspiring form of devotion when she could have recommended something like Bible reading, good books, or even frequent attendance at Mass.

Finally, an attentive friend tried to clue me in on the point of the Rosary. He informed me that the point was to meditate on the mysteries *while* reciting the vocal prayers. I tried doing it—many times—but could not make head or tail of it. How was I to concentrate on the spiritual content of, say, the birth of Jesus or his crucifixion, and at the same time think about the vocal prayers I was saying? It all seemed to me like an impossible form of mental gymnastics! When I asked my pious godfather about this conflict, he just looked at me pityingly but could not find anything helpful to say. Perhaps he thought I still had Protestant tendencies!

It was clearly a no-go situation, so I turned back with some relief to my Marian Office. Like my later mentor, Dorothy Day, I found it "the best thing possible . . . Bits of it keep running through your mind . . . I know that it is constantly lifting me out of trouble."[1]

What I did not realize at the time was that I was experiencing perhaps the lowest point of the Rosary's existence. Strangely enough, for all the emphasis on saying it, apparently few people knew how to pray it well. As far as I could discern, there was no pious literature on the subject. Nobody suggested anything for me to read on *how* to pray the Rosary—except for one priest.

I met Father Donald Hessler at the Detroit Catholic Worker. He had been a Maryknoll missionary in

China before the Communist Revolution and more recently in Mexico. I made a Catholic Worker retreat at their farm in rural Michigan with Father Hessler as the spiritual director. The very first evening with him began to change my attitude toward the Rosary. Before we started its recitation he did a little explaining—a first!—and then asked five different people to make a brief extemporaneous meditation on one of the five mysteries. Some reflected on the event itself, some on its spiritual content, and others on how to apply a mystery to our lives. It was a revelation to me, and from it I learned that the vocal prayers were the less important part of the Rosary and the meditation and application of the mysteries its most significant part.

There remained, however, the same old problem of how to combine the one with the other. Little by little I came to the realization that I was not alone. Far from it, as a matter of fact.

As a college student and then as a college teacher, I found that a myriad of Catholic children had been turned off by the Rosary as it was commonly recited and often abandoned it as soon as they were away from home. They simply found it too tiresome and with little or no spiritual impact. Finding myself in such puzzling company, I too simply let it slide again.

Only much later in life, after discovering something of its history and theology, did I return to it with renewed interest and insight. This book is my attempt at drawing you into the mystery and power of the Rosary as it is meant to be prayed.

Devotion to the Blessed Virgin Mary

The first thing we have to appreciate is that devotion to the Virgin Mary is the touchstone of Catholic orthodoxy. To be devoted to her means that we understand her incomparable role in salvation history, and that as a result we feel drawn to love her, thank her, and pray to her as our loving mother.

The earliest surviving prayer to Mary comes from second-century Egypt and addresses her in this way:

> We turn to you for protection
>   holy Mother of God.
>   Listen to our prayers

and help us in our needs.
Save us from every danger,
glorious and blessed Virgin.[2]

Note her essential title: in the original Greek,
Theotokos; in English, the "One Who Bears God" or,
simply, "Mother of God." Some people are surprised,
even put off, by this her most accurate of titles. And
yet it is her definitive title because it safeguards the
full truth of the incarnation of the Word of God.
It has always been hard to grasp the complete truth
about Jesus because he is fully divine and fully
human at the same time and indissolubly one person.
In the wonderful words of the Nicene Creed, Jesus
is "the only Son of God, eternally begotten of the
Father, God from God, Light from Light, true God
from true God, begotten, not made, of one Being
with the Father" and at the same time "he became
incarnate of the Virgin Mary and was made man."

Great saints, mystics, and theologians have
struggled to comprehend and express this central
mystery—and without full success, since it is literally ineffable. It is "the mystery of faith" by which

we learn to love what we cannot grasp or state with complete accuracy in human words. The might and majesty of the Word made flesh is just too much for our limited minds and words.

One of the classic ways the Church has discovered to protect the great truth about Jesus is by recognizing Mary as *Theotokos* and by invoking her under that supreme title. We cannot stray from the central truths of the Catholic creed if we pray to the Mother of God in full faith and fervor. In actual fact, of course, this title is more about Jesus than it is about Mary. It is a case of Marian theology and devotion stating in faith and prayer what we believe about Jesus himself. It is Mariology anchoring Christology.

In his book, *The Priestly Life*, Ronald Knox writes: "Clearly, the great Christological heresies of the fourth and fifth centuries did much to concentrate attention on our Lady as the hinge, without which our view of the hypostatic union can get no leverage. If our Lord was born, not merely from her, but of her, then he was truly Man. If he was at the same time truly God, then she was, and must be called, the Mother of God. Hence her title of *Theotokos;* she becomes a theological symbol of the utmost importance, and she takes the highest rank accordingly."[3]

When we pray the words, "We turn to you for protection," we stand in the mainstream of sound, orthodox, and Catholic piety. Besides a sound Christology we affirm the marvelous teaching of the communion of saints and, preeminently, of the Virgin Mother of God.

Mary of Nazareth, the holy Mother of God, and devotion to her stand at the heart of Catholic theology and piety and are flourishing in the Catholic and Orthodox churches. The sources and causes are many: the draw of traditional practices in themselves, the liturgical feasts that express Marian theology and piety, the numerous worldwide shrines that draw millions of pilgrims every year, famous Marian apparitions of the nineteenth and twentieth centuries, the role of Mary as expressed by the Second Vatican Council and recent papal teaching, and a fresh vision of long-standing ways of praying that renders them more accessible and more attractive. The finest of these is the Apostolic Letter of Pope John Paul II,

Rosarium Virginis Mariae, issued on October 16, 2002, and expressing his desire to renew the Rosary devotion. It is the most up-to-date, inspiring, and helpful teaching on the Rosary presently available.

Early Witnesses to the Role of Mary

The first witness is the New Testament itself. In the first two chapters of St. Luke's Gospel, Mary's role is set forth beautifully and powerfully, and his portrayal of the Annunciation and the birth of Jesus remains fundamental to all Marian theology. The next witnesses appear in the second century and reveal the beginnings of the steady growth of Marian devotion. Since the middle of the second century, Mary has been called the New Eve and portrayed as the mother of all the living.

St. Justin Martyr (ca. 100–ca. 165) is our first witness to the Eve-Mary parallel:

> Christ is born of the Virgin, in order that the disobedience caused by the serpent might be

destroyed in the same manner in which it had originated. For Eve, an undefiled virgin, conceived the word of the serpent, and brought forth disobedience and death. But the Virgin Mary, filled with faith and joy, when the angel Gabriel announced to her the good tidings that the Spirit of the Lord would come upon her, and the power of the Most High would overshadow her, and therefore the Holy One born of her would be the Son of God, answered: "Be it done unto me according to your word."[4]

Our second witness is St. Irenaeus of Lyons (ca. 125–ca. 202):

Mary the Virgin is found obedient, saying, "Behold the handmaid of the Lord, be it done unto me according to your word" (Luke 1:38). But Eve was disobedient; for she did not obey when as yet she was a virgin, and having become disobedient, was made the cause of death both to herself and the whole human race. So also did Mary . . . by yielding obedience, become the cause of salvation, both to herself and the whole human race . . . And thus also it was that the knot of Eve's disobedience was loosed by the obedience of Mary. For what the virgin Eve had bound through unbelief, this did the Virgin Mary set free through faith.[5]

Another early witness to the Eve-Mary parallel is Tertullian of Carthage (ca. 160–ca. 225), the first of the Latin Fathers:

Just as the death-creating word of the devil had penetrated Eve, who was still a virgin, analogously the life-building Word of God had to enter into a Virgin, so that he who had fallen into perdition because of a woman might be led back to salvation by means of the same sex. Eve believed the serpent; Mary believed Gabriel. The fault that Eve introduced by believing, Mary, by believing, erased.[6]

St. Augustine of Hippo (354–430), the greatest of the Latin Fathers, continued this Eve-Mary parallel:

> Mary is the flower of the field from whom arose the precious lily of the valley through whose birth the wounded nature that we inherited from our first parents is transformed and our sins blotted out. Eve mourned, Mary rejoiced. Eve bore tears in her womb, Mary bore joy, for Eve gave birth to sinners, Mary to the Innocent One. The mother of our race introduced punishment into the world, the Mother of our Lord brought salvation into the world. Eve was the author of sin, Mary the author of merit. By killing, Eve was an obstacle to us, by giving life, Mary was a help. Eve wounded us, Mary healed us. Disobedience is replaced by obedience, faith compensates for unbelief. Mary's canticle puts an end to the lamentations of Eve.[7]

Unlike the primitive Eve who appears in the Genesis story as both the author of life and the bringer of spiritual death to all humanity, Mary is the foundation stone of the new humanity in the order of grace, the bringer of new life in Christ Jesus, and the life-giving mother of the church and of every member of it.

The story of the self-revelation of God to this tiny planet of ours is the almost unbelievable story of the Creator of the universe, of the God of 100 billion galaxies, of a God so immense and all-encompassing that we literally cannot imagine such a Being coming to us in the womb of the Virgin Mary. On a day that must have made the universe tremble, this teenage girl of an obscure Jewish family of Nazareth in Galilee was confronted by an angelic messenger of the Lord who summoned her to a magnificent destiny. Whatever her lowliness in the family and society of her time and the improbability of the message brought to her, she risked everything and freely consented to the overshadowing of the Most High God. The Gospel of Luke shows her to us as at first fearful and doubting and then as entirely at God's disposal. In perfect freedom she chose to obey the divine call: "Here am I, the servant of the Lord; let it be with me according to your word" (Luke 1:38).

Like the prophets of Israel, she listened in fear and trembling to the angelic messenger but accepted the good news brought to her. At that moment she conceived the Son of the Most High, the heir of the promises made to his ancestor King David, the one to be named Jesus, "He who saves." The whole universe must indeed have paused for a moment as it awaited her free consent to the angelic invitation.

In the words of St. Proclus of Constantinople (d. 446), a fearless champion of the Incarnation and of Mary's essential role in bringing it about:

Who ever saw, who ever heard of God in his infinity dwelling in a womb? Heaven cannot contain him, yet a womb cannot constrict him. He was born of woman, but not solely God, man but not merely man. By his birth what once was the door of sin was made the gate of salvation. Through ears that disobeyed, the serpent poured in his poison; through ears that obeyed, the Word entered to form a living temple. In the first case it was Cain, the first pupil of sin, who emerged; in the second it was Christ, the redeemer of the race, who sprouted unsown into life.[8]

Or we can turn to the writings of St. John of Damascus (ca. 675–ca. 749), the author of the first great summary of theology to appear in either the East or the West:

We proclaim the holy Virgin to be properly and truly Mother of God (*Theotokos*). For, as He who was born of her is true God, so she is truly the Mother of God who gave birth to the true God who took flesh from her. Now, we do not say that God was born of her in the sense that the divinity of the Word has its beginning from her, but in the sense that God the Word Himself, who was timelessly begotten of the Father before the ages and exists without beginning and eternally with the Father and the Holy Spirit, did in the last days come for our salvation to dwell in her womb and of her, was, without undergoing change, made flesh and born. For the holy Virgin did not give birth to a mere man but to true God, and not to God simply, but to God made flesh. And He did not bring His body down from heaven and come through her as through a channel, but assumed from her a body consubstantial with us and subsisting in Himself.[9]

For Mary the risk must have been enormous. Even today in a Mediterranean village a girl who gets pregnant outside of wedlock risks not only ostracism but also death. Matthew shows us Joseph, Mary's fiancé, deeply troubled by his pregnant wife-to-be and prepared to put her away quietly rather than expose her to public disgrace and possible death. Only an angelic messenger could persuade him that Mary had not been unfaithful and that the child in her womb was of the Holy Spirit and would be the One who saves (Matthew 1:18–25).

Like Judith of old who became God's instrument to foil the enemies of Israel, Mary cooperated with the Almighty to foil the enemy of the human race and to become even more than Judith, who was "blessed by the Most High God above all other women on earth" (Judith 13:18). What is said of Judith may also be said of Mary: "Your praise will never depart from the hearts of those who remember the power of God. May God grant this to be perpetual honor to you, and may he reward you with blessings, because you risked your own life and averted our ruin" (Judith 13:18–20). In the end, however, Mary, much more than Judith, became "the glory of Jerusalem, the great boast of Israel, the pride of our nation" (Judith 15:9).

Mary's cousin Elizabeth put it this way: "Blessed are you among women, and blessed is the fruit of your womb" (Luke 1:42). But more than Elizabeth could have possibly comprehended, Mary became, properly speaking, the *Theotokos*, the Mother of God. From as early as the late second century, piety and theological reflection gave her this accurate title in order to safeguard the full mystery of the Incarnation, of the union of the divine and human natures in a single person, the Lord Christ.

As they meditated on the Father's gift of Jesus to us, early Christian believers came to see more and more the supreme role Mary played in giving birth to the God-man and through him to the People of God.

The heartfelt sentiments represented in "We turn to you for protection" have lasted from the second to the twenty-first century. In virtue of her total gift of herself to the plan of God for our salvation, Mary is the first believer, the first Christian, the model of the believing church and of each believing person. In virtue of the mystery of the church whereby we are all united in the Body of Christ, she listens to our prayers, helps us in our needs, and saves us from every danger. She is indeed the "glorious and blessed Virgin!"

One of the finest results of the theological debates in the fourth and fifth centuries on how to explain and state accurately the two natures in Christ, was the emergence of Mary's title *Theotokos* in its deepest significance. Not only does it help believers to grasp the fullness of the Incarnation, it also sets the Mother of God in her rightful place in the economy of salvation. It resulted in a fuller and more inclusive piety toward Mary that produced in her name a wealth of churches, sermons, hymns, poems, homilies, pilgrimage centers, and an unending stream of popular devotions and liturgies characteristic of the eastern and western churches of the ancient world and of our own time.

Here is what St. Ephrem of Syria (d. 373), "the harp of the Holy Spirit," had to say of the *Theotokos:*

> Mary bore a mute Babe
> though in Him were hidden all our tongues.
> Joseph carried Him, yet hidden in Him was
> a silent nature older than everything.
> The Lofty One became like a little child,
> yet hidden in Him was
> a treasure of Wisdom that suffices for all.
> He was lofty but He sucked Mary's milk,
> and from His blessings all creation sucks.
> He is the Living Breast of living breath;

by His life the dead were suckled, and they
    revived.
Without the breath of air no one can live;
without the power of the Son no one can rise.
Upon the living breath of the One who
    vivifies all
depend the living beings above and below.
As indeed He sucked Mary's milk,
He has given suck-life to the universe.
As again He dwelt in His mother's womb,
in His womb dwells all creation.
Mute He was as a babe, yet he gave
to all creation all his commands.[10]

Or, again, hear how St. Proclus of Constantinople
exalted the role of the *Theotokos:*

Holy Mary . . . awe-inspiring loom of God's
saving plan, on which the garment of unity
was indescribably woven, whose weaver is the
Holy Spirit, and whose spinner is the overshadowing power from on high, whose wool
is the old sheepskin of Adam; the warp is the

immaculate flesh of the Virgin, the shuttle the measureless grace of her who bore him, and the designer is the Word, who entered her by hearing.[11]

What had been introduced so significantly in the mid-fourth century by St. Ephrem in his Syriac hymns and verse homilies and in the early fifth century by St. Proclus, patriarch of Constantinople, in his Greek homilies, became a continuous theme in the magnificent homilies of the Greek Fathers and their theological descendants.

The orthodox tradition culminated in St. John of Damascus (ca. 675–ca. 749). His three homilies on the Dormition of Mary delivered during the vigil of August 15, in the 730s or 740s, portray Mary's falling asleep in death and her bodily assumption as the crowning glory of her service of love to our incarnate Savior.

It was fitting that she, who preserved her virginity undamaged by childbirth, should have her body preserved from corruption even in death. It was fitting that she, who held the Creator in her lap as a baby, should rest in the tabernacle of God. It was fitting that the bride, whom the Father took for his own, should dwell in the bridal-chamber of heaven. It was fitting that she, who gazed at her son on the cross, and who [there] received in her heart the sword of pain she escaped in child-birth, should look on him enthroned with his Father. It was fitting that the Mother of God should receive the blessings of her son, and be reverenced by all creation as Mother and servant of God.[12]

The Church of the East Roman Empire also expressed the definitive Christology of the Ecumenical Councils of Ephesus (431) and Chalcedon (451) in fervent religious poetry that endures through the present. The beautiful *Akathistos Hymn* or *Exaltation of the Mother of God* was composed in the fifth century for the new feast of the Annunciation (March 25) and is considered "the most beautiful, the most profound, the most ancient Marian hymn in all Christian literature." It soon became a part of the Byzantine Liturgy and of all its daughter churches. It is still sung publicly in the Byzantine Rite during Lent and is used with great frequency as a private devotion.[13]

The opening lines illustrate the character of this exultant hymn:

KONTAKION 1
Queen of the Heavenly Host, Defender of our souls, we your servants offer to you songs of victory and thanksgiving, for you, O Mother of God, have delivered us from all dangers. But as you have invincible power, free us from conflicts of all kinds that we may cry to you:
Rejoice, unwedded Bride!

EIKOS 1
An Archangel was sent from heaven to say to the Mother of God: Rejoice! And seeing you, O Lord, taking bodily form, he was amazed and with his bodiless voice he stood crying to her such things as these:

Rejoice, you through whom joy will flash
        forth!
Rejoice, you through whom the curse will
        cease!
Rejoice, revival of fallen Adam!
Rejoice, redemption of the tears of Eve!
Rejoice, height hard to climb for human
        thoughts!
Rejoice, depth hard to contemplate even
        for the eyes of angels!
Rejoice, you who are the King's throne!
Rejoice, you who bear him who bears all!
Rejoice, star that caused the Sun to appear!
Rejoice, womb of the divine incarnation!
Rejoice, you through whom creation
        becomes new!
Rejoice, you through whom the Creator
        becomes a babe!
Rejoice, unwedded Bride![14]

The repeated "Rejoice" (*chaire* in Greek) recalls, of course, the salutation of the Archangel Gabriel to the Blessed Virgin (Luke 1:28) as he brought her the good news of the Divine Incarnation and of her role in it. As in the case of the later Western Rosary, this form of salutation was used with epithets of various kinds to set forth the reasons for saluting Mary and her divine Child.

In addition to the poetry and homilies of the Fathers, the other magnificent testimonies to the triumph of orthodoxy were the new Marian churches established in Jerusalem, New Rome (Constantinople), and Old Rome on the Tiber. The first church was built at the foot of the Mount of Olives, near Gethsemane, the source of the Virgin's preeminent feast of August 15; others were erected in Constantinople by the virgin-empress Pulcheria (399–453) to house some of Mary's precious relics; and in Rome itself Pope Sixtus III (432–440) restored the magnificent basilica, Saint Mary Major, to commemorate the Council of Ephesus (431) and its precious teaching on the incarnate Christ.

Marian Devotion in the Latin West

Perhaps because the controversies over the dual nature of Christ were not quite so pressing in the western Mediterranean, the development of Marian feasts, theology, and devotions were slower to appear in the Latin churches of the West. Rome derived most of its Marian feasts from the East through the intermediary of Greek and Syrian popes of the seventh and eighth centuries, but the various Latin churches soon learned how to venerate the Virgin Mother in their own way.

Early on the Latin churches of Spain and Gaul had created a Marian feast of the Incarnation on December 18, and Rome itself instituted its first Marian festival on January 1 to commemorate the Virgin Mary's indispensable role in the birth of Christ.

Here is the witness of St. CuChuimne, a Celtic monk of Iona (ca. 747), to Our Lady:

In alternate measure chanting, daily sing we
  Mary's praise,

And in strain of glad rejoicing, to the Lord
    our voices raise.

With a twofold choir repeating, Mary's never
    dying fame,
Let each ear the praises gather, which our
    grateful tongues proclaim.

Judah's ever glorious daughter—chosen
    mother of the Lord—
Who, to weak and fallen manhood, all its
    ancient worth restored.

From the everlasting Father, Gabriel brought
    the glad decree,
That the Word divine conceiving, she should
    set poor sinners free.

Of all virgins pure, the purest—ever
    stainless, ever bright—
Still from grace to grace advancing—fairest
    daughter of the light.

Wondrous title—who shall tell it—whilst the
    Word divine she bore
Though in mother's name rejoicing, virgin
    purer than before!

By a woman's disobedience, eating the
    forbidden tree,
Was the world betray'd and ruin'd—was by
    woman's aid set free.

In mysterious mode a mother, Mary did her
    God conceive,
By whose grace, through saving waters, men
    did heavenly truth receive.

By no empty dreams deluded, for the pearl
    which Mary bore
Men, all earthly wealth resigning, still are
    rich for evermore.

For her Son a seamless tunic Mary's careful
    hand did weave;
O'er that tunic fiercely gambling, sinners
    Mary's heart did grieve.

Clad in helmet of salvation—clad in
    breastplate shining bright—
May the hand of Mary guide us to the
    realms of endless light.

Amen, amen, loudly cry we—may she when
    the fight is won,

O'er avenging fires triumphing, lead us safely
to her Son.

Holy angels gathering round us, lo, His
saving name we greet,
Writ in books of life eternal, may we still
that name repeat.[15]

The Marian Votive Mass

By the ninth century we find the votive Mass of
the Blessed Virgin that came to be celebrated on
Saturdays throughout the whole Latin Church.
It was composed by Blessed Alcuin of York (ca.
735–804), the famous Carolingian scholar and
abbot, and contained the foundational collect prayer
that endures even into the twenty-first century:
"*Concede nos famulos tuos*, Lord God, grant us your
servants continuing health of mind and body and
by the intercession of the glorious and ever-Virgin
Mary, free us from present sorrow and conduct us
into eternal joy; through our Lord Jesus Christ your

Son, who lives and reigns with you and the Holy Spirit, one God, for ever and ever. Amen."[16]

The Marian Office

In the next century, the private piety of a saintly bishop like Ulrich of Augsburg (890–973) created one of the first votive Offices of Mary, a form of devotion that spread through monasteries, cathedrals, and new orders of friars until it became the most popular form of devotion to Mary in the medieval church.

This devotional expression of Marian piety took a quite different form than that of Eastern liturgies and devotions. It originated as a small, daily attachment to the Night Office but gradually became a complete Office in its own right. Its eight daily services of hymns, psalms, lessons, canticles, and prayers paralleled and complemented those of the Divine Office proper. The Marian Office, however, was almost invariable, having the same components every day; it could be carried about in a small pocketbook and easily memorized, and was often recited rather than sung. In monasteries and cathedrals it was usually recited just before each hour of the regular office and was only omitted on the high feast days of Mary and during Holy Week and Easter Week.[17]

As in the case of so many popular devotions, what began in monasteries soon became a devotion of lay-people. Its brevity and invariability commended itself to laypeople, and it could be prayed either in Latin or a vernacular language. In the following centuries the Little Office of the Blessed Virgin became the essential nucleus of the famous Books of Hours that spread everywhere and became *the* prayer book of the literate laity for the rest of the Middle Ages. Even in a period of widespread illiteracy, Books of Hours were best sellers and continued to hold their place of honor, century after century.[18]

The Hail Mary Devotion

The text of the popular Little Office of Mary influenced the development of other forms of Marian

devotion and became the remote ancestor of the
Rosary. The best indication of this is how the opening lines of Matins became a salutation devotion in
their own right. This first hour of the day (Matins)
opened with the invitatory verse, "Hail, Mary, full
of grace, the Lord is with you," and this verse of
Scripture was repeated several times during the
recitation of Psalm 95, the call to prayer that began
the daily Office.

This greeting could be easily excerpted from
the Marian Office and used by itself to salute the
Blessed Virgin in the mystery of the Annunciation.
This was done by repeating the Hail Mary in this
short form numerous times—often 50, 100, or 150
times—with a genuflection or prostration at each
repetition. This was an easy way of immersing one-
self in the mystery of the Word made flesh and in
Mary's joy at becoming the Mother of the Messiah.
It was therefore both a convenient Christological
and Mariological devotion.

Here is the example of St. Louis IX, King of
France (1214–1270) who "knelt down every day
fifty times in the evening, and each time he stood

upright again and then knelt down anew, and each time he knelt down he said very slowly an Ave Maria."[19]

Sometime later, there emerged a fuller form of the Hail Mary salutation by adding the further greeting of Mary's cousin Elizabeth: "Blessed are you among women, and blessed is the fruit of your womb" (Luke 1:42). By the twelfth century the name of Mary had been inserted in the original scriptural phrase, and by the fourteenth century the holy name of Jesus was added by way of conclusion to its fuller form. That was the complete Hail Mary known to the Middle Ages and therefore to the Rosary when it appeared in the fifteenth century.

It was only in the sixteenth century that a final petition was added to the name of Jesus: "Holy Mary, Mother of God, pray for us sinners, now and at the hour of our death. Amen."

And yet the popular Office of Mary and the salutation devotion of repeated Hail Marys did not exhaust the pious aspirations of the Christian Middle Ages. Soon a newer and longer form of the Hail Mary devotion appeared.

The Ave Psalter

Originating in religious houses as early as the twelfth century in both Latin and the vernacular, the new devotion, known as the Ave Psalter, had a versified Marian antiphon before each of the 150 psalms. Each stanza began with the first words of the Hail Mary (Ave Maria) and continued with a title of honor and two lines of prayer related to the psalm at hand:

Here are three examples attributed to the learned and eloquent theologian Stephen Langton, Archbishop of Canterbury (ca. 1150–1228):

Psalm 1: *Beatus vir*
Hail, Virgin of virgins, mother without peer,
Worthy to conceive without a man's help:
Help us *meditate on the law of the Lord*
And arrive at the blessedness of the glorious
kingdom.

Psalm 2: *Quare fremuerunt gentes*
Hail, whose womb brought forth a Son,
Against whom *the nations raged*.

Listen to the voices of those who call on you,
Removing the causes of evil that have
befallen us.

Psalm 6: *Domine, ne in furore tuo*
Hail, gate of life, salvation of the penitent,
Look upon the miseries of a feeble soul.
Lest I sense an angry and accusing voice
Take away both my sins and my
punishment.[20]

The Emerging Rosary

As time passed, these miscellaneous stanzas were separated from the psalms themselves and became autonomous poems of praise and petition to the Virgin. As important and popular as these were, a newly developed focus on the life of Jesus drew various authors to attach epithets to the Hail Mary in a logical sequence, thus drawing us closer to the birth of the Rosary proper. Once the custom of saluting Mary by reciting a series of 50 or 150 Hail Marys was united with short clauses or tags attached to each bead, the Rosary of the fifteenth century came into being.

Now the Hail Mary took a form like this:

Hail, Mary full of grace, the Lord is with you.
Blessed are you among women
and blessed is the fruit of your womb, Jesus,
who was conceived in your womb
at the message of an angel.

The words in italics changed with each Hail Mary, meaning that if fifty Hail Marys were recited, there were fifty accompanying clauses covering the main features of the life of Jesus. As printed books became popular, such *clausulae* (tags or phrases) were printed out and read off after the word Jesus to conclude each Hail Mary.

The Golden Rosary

This way of reciting the Rosary has endured through the present in various European dioceses, and especially in Germany. A typical example appears in the pilgrim prayer book of the diocese of Trier published in 1933. Here is a translation of the introduction and the clauses of the first decade:

> Praised and blest be the name of our Lord
>   Jesus Christ
> and the name of the glorious Virgin Mary for
>   ever and ever!

The Apostles' Creed

Lord, have mercy. Christ, have mercy. Lord, have mercy.

The Lord's Prayer and ten Hail Marys. After the word JESUS the following phrases are added:

- whom you conceived by the Holy Spirit
- with whom you went with haste to visit your cousin Elizabeth
- to whom you gave birth in Bethlehem of Judea

- whom you wrapped in bands of cloth, and laid in a manger
- whom the angels proclaimed to the shepherds
- whom the shepherds found in a manger
- who was called Jesus at his circumcision, the eighth day after his birth
- whom the Magi adored and honored with gold, frankincense, and myrrh
- whom you offered in the temple to the heavenly Father
- with whom you fled into Egypt and returned to Nazareth[21]

This development is attributed to the Carthusian monk, Dominic Eloyns of Prussia (1384–1460) of the Trier Charterhouse, although recent discoveries reveal that others had preceded him in this fortunate innovation. Dominic and his fellow hermits, however, were the great disseminators of the new Rosary of fifty Hail Marys with attached clauses related to the life of Christ. The older salutation devotion to Mary in the mystery of the Incarnation was now subsumed into the fifty mysteries of the life of Christ—and that meant a fully intertwined Christological and Marian devotion.[22]

In all this we have to remember that popular devotions are not usually standardized for a long time. And this proved especially true of the Rosary devotion. There were many different kinds of rosaries prevalent in the late Middle Ages, but only one form, called the new Rosary, became *the* Rosary as we know it.

As a boy I inherited a rosary of sixty-three beads from my French-Canadian great-grandmother. This six-decade form puzzled me at first until I learned about the rosary of St. Bride (Bridgid) of Sweden (1303–1373). She was a fourteenth-century Swedish mystic famous for her visions and revelations, and her Rosary stems from one of her visions in which she saw that Mary lived to be sixty-three years old. It had no clauses attached to the Hail Marys because they were recited as salutations in the older manner. One survival of this form of Rosary is the group of three Hail Marys still attached to the beginning of the now standard Rosary.

With fifty Hail Marys divided into decades by the Lord's Prayer and the addition of Life of Christ meditations, we are getting nearer and nearer to the Rosary as we now know it. The next innovation was in part the result of a technical advance, the appearance of printed Rosary booklets with woodcuts that presented images of the major joyous, sorrowful, and glorious events set forth in the Rosary. The first book of this kind was printed and illustrated for the Rosary Brotherhood of Ulm in 1483. It had no text to go with the pictures, but these could be easily "read" even by those who could not decipher a printed text. Stained glass windows, altar carvings, and paintings combined with sermons abounded in medieval churches, and especially in Germany. It was no great leap to produce small printed booklets to illustrate the mysteries of the Rosary.[23]

The Classic Rosary

Just how the new form of the Rosary came into being and grew to replace practically all its other forms is a rather complicated matter. Suffice it to say that various Dominican directors of the popular Confraternity of the Rosary experimented with the forms of the Rosary they knew and eventually came up with the classic Rosary of fifteen mysteries, fifteen recitations of the Lord's Prayer, fifteen decades of Hail Marys with attached clauses, and, ultimately, fifteen Glorias. It is possible that the origin of reciting the Gloria at the end of each decade derives from the Dominican practice of singing the Rosary in choir at the Minerva, the international headquarters of the Order of Preachers in Rome.

Although other forms of the Rosary eventually came into being—notably that of the Seven Joys of Mary (Franciscans) and that of the Seven Sorrows of Mary (Servites of Mary)—the so-called Dominican Rosary became widely known as simply *the* Rosary. This meditated life-of-Christ Rosary became increasingly popular during the Catholic Reformation era and in the new religious orders like the Jesuits. In 1569 the Dominican pope, St. Pius V, approved this form of the Rosary in its now classic shape, granted indulgences for its

recitation, and encouraged its devout use throughout the Catholic world.

Decline of the Meditated Rosary

Unfortunately, with the passage of time, the Rosary
lost its more meditative character by dropping the
clauses attached to each Hail Mary and by neglect-
ing the illustrated Rosary booklets. It tended to
become merely fifteen decades of vocal prayers "in
honor of" the fifteen mysteries. Even so famous
an apostle of Mary and the Rosary as St. Louis de
Montfort (1673–1716), who composed meditations
for each mystery, could not stem the tide of the more
mechanical recitation. Such a curtailing of the most
important part of the Rosary explains why I and so
many other Catholics found the Rosary to be a less
than satisfying form of devotion. Nevertheless, this
unhappy situation is now being reversed both by
the work of modern historians of piety and by the
opportune intervention of Pope John Paul II.

The Basic Vocal Prayers
of the Rosary

In its commonest form, each chaplet (five decades) of the full Rosary is introduced by the sign of the Cross, the recitation of the Apostles' Creed, the Lord's Prayer, and three Hail Marys for the three theological virtues of faith, hope, and charity. Then each decade is introduced by the announcement of a mystery and succeeded by a Lord's Prayer, ten Hail Marys, and a Gloria Patri. Each chaplet is often concluded by a Marian anthem and prayer and/or by the Litany of Loreto.

The Sign of the Cross

This holy sign is given to us in Baptism when our foreheads are sealed with chrism. We use it frequently in its small version (at the Holy Gospel) and in its larger version at Mass, in the Liturgy of the Hours, in all the sacraments, and in most private prayers and popular devotions.

> In the name † of the Father,
> and of the Son,
> and of the Holy Spirit. Amen.

The Apostles' Creed

This statement is the most fundamental act of our baptismal faith and commitment to its promises.

> I believe in God, the Father almighty,
> creator of heaven and earth.

I believe in Jesus Christ, God's only Son, our
      Lord,
   who was conceived by the Holy Spirit,
   born of the Virgin Mary,
   suffered under Pontius Pilate,
   was crucified, died, and was buried;
   he descended to the dead.
   On the third day he rose again;
   he ascended into heaven,
   he is seated at the right hand of the
      Father,
   and he will come to judge the living and
      the dead.

I believe in the Holy Spirit,
   the holy catholic Church,
   the communion of saints,
   the forgiveness of sins,
   the resurrection of the body,
   and the life everlasting. Amen.[24]

The Lord's Prayer

The Lord's Prayer was given to the disciples of Jesus by the Lord himself and is both a pattern of prayer and a prayer itself.

Modern Version
Our Father in heaven,
hallowed be your name,
your kingdom come,
your will be done,
on earth as in heaven.
Give us today our daily bread.
Forgive us our sins
as we forgive those who sin against us.
Save us from the time of trial
and deliver us from evil.
For the kingdom, the power, and the glory
    are yours
now and for ever. Amen.[25]

Older Version
Our Father, who art in heaven,

hallowed be thy name;

thy kingdom come;

thy will be done on earth as it is in heaven.

Give us this day our daily bread;

and forgive us our trespasses

as we forgive those who trespass against us;

and lead us not into temptation,

but deliver us from evil.

For thine is the kingdom and the power and

     the glory,

for ever and ever. Amen.

"After listening to the word and focusing on the mystery, it is natural for *the mind to be lifted up towards the Father.* In each of his mysteries, Jesus always leads us to the Father, for as he rests in the Father's bosom (John 1:18) he is continually turned towards him. He wants us to share in his intimacy with the Father, so that we can say with him: 'Abba, Father' (Romans 8:15). Acting as a kind of foundation of the Christological and Marian meditation which unfolds in the repetition of the Hail Mary, the Our Father

makes meditation upon the mystery, even when carried out in solitude, an ecclesial experience."

Pope John Paul II,
Rosarium Virginis Mariae, # 32

The Hail Mary

The Hail Mary is composed of two greetings to
the Virgin Mary from St. Luke's account of the
Annunciation (1:28) and the Visitation (1:42) and of
a final prayer of petition composed by the church.

"The center of gravity in the Hail Mary, the
hinge as it were which joins its two parts, is *the
name of Jesus.* Sometimes, in hurried recitation, this
center of gravity can be overlooked, and with it the
connection to the mystery of Christ being contemplated. Yet it is precisely the emphasis given to
the name of Jesus that is the sign of a meaningful
and fruitful recitation of the Rosary. Pope Paul VI
drew attention to the custom in certain regions of

highlighting the name of Christ by the addition of a clause referring to the mystery being contemplated. This is a praiseworthy custom, especially during public recitation. It gives forceful expression to our faith in Christ, directed to the different moments of the Redeemer's life. It is at once a profession of faith and an aid in concentrating our meditation, since it facilitates the process of assimilation to the mystery of Christ inherent in the repetition of the Hail Mary."

Pope John Paul II,
Rosarium Virginis Mariae, # 33

Hail, Mary, full of grace, the Lord is with you.
Blessed are you among women,
   and blessed is the fruit of your womb, JESUS.
Holy Mary, Mother of God, pray for us
         sinners,
      now and at the hour of our death. Amen.

Some may prefer a more recent translation of the angel's salutation (Luke 1:28).

Greetings, favored one!
The Lord is with you. (NRSV)

Hail, favored one!
The Lord is with you. (NAB)

Or these versions:

Rejoice, you who enjoy God's favor!
The Lord is with you. (NJB)

Greetings, gracious Lady!
The Lord is with you.

"As a Gospel prayer, centered on the mystery of the redemptive Incarnation, the Rosary is a prayer with a clearly Christological orientation. Its most characteristic element, in fact, the litany-like succession of Hail Marys, becomes in itself an unceasing praise of Christ, who is the ultimate object both of the Angel's announcement and of the greeting of the mother of John the Baptist: 'Blessed is the fruit of your womb' (Luke 1:42)."

Pope John Paul II,
Rosarium Virginis Mariae, # 18

Doxology: The Gloria Patri

Glory to the Father, and to the Son,
and to the Holy Spirit:
as it was in the beginning, is now,
and will be for ever. Amen.

"Trinitarian doxology is the goal of all Christian contemplation. For Christ is the way that leads us to the Father in the Spirit. If we travel this way to the end, we repeatedly encounter the mystery of the three divine Persons, to whom all praise, worship, and thanksgiving are due. It is important that *the Gloria Patri, the high point of contemplation*, be given due prominence in the Rosary. In public celebration it could be sung, as a way of giving proper emphasis to the essentially Trinitarian structure of all Christian prayer."

Pope John Paul II,
Rosarium Virginis Mariae, #34

Praying the Rosary with Adults

Pope John Paul II's *Rosariun Virginis Mariae* (October 15, 2002) introduces a new program for the Rosary that draws on its earlier history, adds five Luminous Mysteries to the original fifteen, and suggests a variety of ways to enhance how we pray it. By following his inspiring teaching I believe the boredom and lassitude that so many people complain of will be diminished, and we will all learn to pray the Rosary better and with greater spiritual results.

Seven papal suggestions must be considered:

1. The use of a picture illustrating each mystery
2. The reading of an appropriate passage from one of the Gospels before each decade

3. The observance of a suitable period of silence after the reading (and/or homily in public recitations)

4. The addition of a scriptural tag after the word JESUS in each Hail Mary

5. The saying or singing of the Gloria Patri at the end of each decade

6. The addition of a final prayer that sums up and applies each mystery

7. The use of one of the Marian anthems and/ or the Litany of Loreto at the conclusion of each chaplet

The overall emphasis is on a measured, calm, reflective recitation, using all the above resources with common sense and discretion.

This Rosary book facilitates the above points by supplying the following:

• Introductory meditations on the four sets of mysteries, taken from Pope John Paul II's pastoral letter and from the *Showings* of Blessed Julian of Norwich

- Twenty pictures (icons) for visual emphasis
- A passage from one of the Gospels for each mystery and other suggested Scripture passages
- A scriptural or liturgical tag for each Hail Mary
- Simple music for a sung Gloria Patri
- A final prayer at the end of each decade
- A traditional Marian anthem for each of the four sets of mysteries
- Other suggested Marian prayers: the Litany of Loreto, the *Te Matrem Laudamus*, and *Obsecro Te*

Private and Public Recitation

Originally, the Rosary was a private devotion prayed by an individual person; for many, this may still be the best way to approach it. Even great saints like Thérèse of Lisieux (1873–1897) found the group recitation of the Rosary very difficult. Maybe, if she had been allowed to pray quietly in her room, she could have enjoyed it as a peaceful form of contemplative prayer. Private recitation allows for more pauses as the Spirit moves us; lets us sigh, groan, weep, or laugh when we feel like it; and permits us to sit, kneel, or stand as we see fit.

In the fifteenth century, the Rosary Confraternities began to recite five decades in common, a trend that spread through both homes and churches. Though widely promoted by apostles of the Rosary, bishops, and popes, Pope John Paul II's suggestions for its improvement will be especially useful.

On retreats and days of recollection, some groups like to have a "walking Rosary" in a garden, cloister, or woods. With the above qualifications, this also could prove useful if it is prayed in a rhythm of quiet walking. Even five decades might not be too lengthy on such occasions.

Weekend retreats are a useful occasion for introducing the renewed Rosary. The whole twenty decades might be prayed at intervals over the course of the weekend. Such a total immersion approach could be related to the liturgical year and explain how the private devotion of the Rosary and the public celebration of the Liturgy complement and enhance each other.

"Every group that gathers to recite the Rosary is a gift for the Kingdom of God. Yes, wherever two or three are gathered in the name of Christ, he is there."

Pope John Paul II[26]

Distribution of the Mysteries over Time

Some people may have the leisure to recite the whole twenty decades of the Rosary each day: the unemployed, the sick, the elderly, retired people with lots of time on their hands, those who find it hard to sleep through the night. But most people will only be able to pray five decades each day, according to a weekly pattern suggested by Pope John Paul II in his *Apostolic Letter*, # 38:

Joyful Mysteries: Monday and Saturday
Luminous Mysteries: Thursday

Sorrowful Mysteries: Tuesday and Friday
Glorious Mysteries: Wednesday and Sunday

Those who cannot find time for a whole chaplet (five decades) each day might consider praying the whole Rosary once a week. If we recite three decades each day, Sunday through Friday, and the last two decades on Saturday, we can easily complete the whole round of the twenty mysteries in a week.

A personal commitment—after due consideration—to use one or another of these methods with regularity could mark the renewal of daily prayer and meditation in a person's life.

Devotion to Jesus and Mary in the form of the Rosary may even lead some people to take a vow to say the whole Rosary once a week. Such a vow may be considered a concrete renewal of one's baptismal vows because, by doing so, we engage ourselves to meditate and carry out in our lives the central mysteries of the Gospel as they appear in the Holy Rosary.

People who pray some form of the Liturgy of the Hours each day may not find the time to pray the Rosary daily. They might, however, consider praying it on Saturdays, on the major feasts of Jesus and Mary, and on other special occasions.

There should be no conflict between one's love for the Liturgy of the Hours and for the Rosary. Both are "a compendium of the Gospel," (Pope Paul VI), spiritual paths that lead us into contemplative prayer and the daily living of the promises made at our baptism.

"The Rosary, though clearly Marian in character, is at heart a Christocentric prayer. With the Rosary, the Christian people *sits at the school of Mary* and is led to contemplate the beauty of the face of Christ and to experience the depths of his love."

Pope John Paul II,
Rosarium Virginis Mariae, # 1

How to Pray the Rosary

Those who have never learned to pray the Rosary need to be introduced to it step by step. My suggestion would be to begin by focusing on one mystery at a time, reciting only one decade, without haste, concentrating mostly on the vocal prayers: the Lord's Prayer, the ten Hail Marys, and the Gloria Patri. By so doing, they will be using one of the original ways of saluting the Blessed Virgin repeatedly in honor of her role in our salvation. It is helpful to say the prayers with the lips—not just mentally—and to use the rosary beads as counters and aids to recollection.

After a time, beginners might insert the Scripture reading after announcing each mystery, pause a bit after reading it for silent reflection, and then say the

Our Father, the ten Hail Marys, the Gloria Patri, and the suggested closing prayer. To *meditate* means to turn over and over in the mind some key phrase that strikes us while we are reading the Gospel passage. Or it can mean focusing on the whole event of the mystery or part of it so that we see it in our mind's eye and let its meaning sink into our soul. By doing so we assimilate the Bible text more fully than by merely reading it.

The next step would be to add the brief clause or clauses that are suggested to go with each Hail Mary. The single clause printed in the text is specifically designed for beginners to use with each Hail Mary before they feel they are ready to proceed to the ten different clauses. After becoming very familiar with the ten clauses, many people will discover that they want to use only one repeatedly, or a few of them for each decade.

What matters most is getting used to saying the vocal prayers while continuing to meditate (at least to some degree) on the mysteries. This will require effort, practice, and patience. Some days we will find ourselves doing more of one than the other. Not to worry! The whole point is to keep in focus the twenty mysteries of redemption as they are revealed in the Gospels. With patience and perseverance everything will fall into place by the assistance of the Holy Spirit who lives in our hearts.

The high points of the vocal prayers themselves are the words "Our Father" in the Lord's Prayer, the holy names of Mary and Jesus in each Hail Mary, and the holy names of the Three Persons of the Blessed Trinity in the Gloria Patri.

Meditation

People who stick with the Rosary will sooner or later find—barring special obstacles— that they are immersing themselves in the mysteries with great joy and devotion. Sometimes the mere announcement of the mystery will set up a kind of spiritual vibration that carries them through the whole decade. At other times just one scene from the mystery will bring out a longing/loving admiration that fills the whole soul. At another time the holy names alone will draw us with such intensity that all other words will fall into the background. Such faithful users of the Rosary will find that they are sinking into the mystery with delight, thanksgiving, and deeper and deeper joy. What is old becomes new and stimulates us to admiration and love. After a while we can leave mere information behind because it is already assimilated. Now we find ourselves more in the realm of feeling, affection, and commitment. We come to grasp the whole of the mystery, not just its parts. Our imagination and intellect—so useful in the beginning—fail before the wealth of emotion and attachment to the inner core of the mystery. Now we have *heartfelt* knowledge—a very special kind of knowledge that brings Jesus and Mary to the fore in a new way. We begin to cross the line between knowing *about* the Lord and knowing Jesus and Mary in person. We learn to stop trying so hard to picture Jesus and Mary in the events of their lives and to reach out to them with love in all the inexplicable fullness of their being.

"To recite the Rosary is nothing other than to *contemplate with Mary the face of Christ.*"

Pope John Paul II,
Rosarium Virginis Mariae, # 3

Contemplation

Little by little we pass from meditation into some form of *contemplation.* This does not mean that we neglect the Gospel reading or the vocal prayers; rather it means that we have drawn them so deeply into our inner being that the *silence* of the Rosary now becomes its main attraction. An overwhelming sense of the divine Presence invades our whole person. We are drawn to rest in the free gift of divine love that is manifested to us in each mystery without any particular considerations on the part of the intellect or imagination. The central fact of our prayer experience now becomes "God is love, and those who abide in love abide in God, and God abides in them" (1 John 4:16). We know, we feel—to use inadequate words—that God *is*, God *exists*, that God is *Emmanuel*, that *God is with us* in Jesus, that the origin and goal of the entire universe is *love*. With the sublime mystic, Julian of Norwich, we come to know that "Love is God's meaning." And our response is a mixture of welcome, gratitude, surrender, and peace. St. Augustine of Hippo once said that we shall spend eternity singing "alleluia" so we had better get used to it now. He knew by experience that contemplative prayer ends in just repeating forever "Praise God!"

"The Rosary belongs among the finest and most praiseworthy traditions of Christian contemplation. Developed in the West, it is a typically meditative prayer, corresponding in some way to 'the prayer of the heart' or 'Jesus prayer' which took root in the soil of the Christian East."

Pope John Paul II,
Rosarium Virginis Mariae, #5

Praying the Rosary with Children

The Family Rosary is a special challenge. To my mind what is needed here is a fairly simple, brief, and illustrated form of the Rosary. Obliging children to pray five decades at one time, on their knees, and without pictorials, is likely to backfire. Younger children especially should concentrate on one decade at a time with the focus on the story of the mystery as told in the parents' own words while the child is seated and viewing a picture of the event in question.

After the story is recounted and while the icon is being viewed, perhaps one Lord's Prayer, *three* Hail Marys, the Gloria Patri, and the closing prayer might suffice. The three Hail Marys might well have an appropriate tag attached to them in order to bring the essence of the mystery to the fore. For example: "Jesus, who was born for us of the Virgin Mary" for the third joyful mystery; "Jesus, who died for us on the cross" for the fifth sorrowful mystery; "Jesus, who crowned his mother Queen of heaven" for the fifth glorious mystery. In the case of children, I feel that "less is more."

Older children are sometimes even more of a problem than younger ones.

The mere rote recitation of a whole chaplet, what Pope John Paul II called "an impoverished method of praying," can drive them away from the Rosary.[27] If we are to get anywhere with them, we will have to teach them how to visualize the mysteries, how to meditate in the sense explained above, and how to advance toward contemplation. This is a true challenge for parents, pastors, retreat directors, and teachers. Unless they themselves have met the inner challenge of the Rosary, they will accomplish little or nothing with children of any age.

Praying the Rosary in the Face of Death and Dying

This is another special challenge. Here, too, one or two decades of the Rosary with appropriate readings from the sorrowful or glorious mysteries might be quite enough. This is especially true of wakes attended largely by people who have little or no experience of the Rosary. I have found that both Catholics and other Christians can be easily offended and turned off by five whole decades without an introduction, readings, silence, meditations, or appropriate prayers. On the other hand, a wake can become an occasion of grace for almost everyone if it is turned into what should be called a Rosary Service: brief introductory remarks followed by a reading from the Gospel and brief homily, silent reflection, the usual vocal prayers recited slowly, and a prayer at the end of the decade that summarizes and applies the mystery to the occasion. See Appendix 2 for suggested prayers for such an occasion.

The Rosary in Church

Holy Hours and Rosary Hours used to be common in North America, but they have declined in many parish churches and religious houses. In this case, too, I would suggest introducing a Rosary Service:

an appropriate opening hymn, a Gospel reading followed by a meditative homily and silent prayer, the usual Our Father and Hail Marys with their tags, a sung Gloria, and a closing prayer. Standing, sitting, or kneeling at appropriate points in this kind of service is an important consideration.

How many decades done in this manner I leave to the common sense of the pastor and his liturgy committee. One of the traditional Marian anthems or the Litany of Loreto may bring the Rosary to an end.

The whole service could well conclude with the Benediction of the Blessed Sacrament and a strong closing hymn.

"The Rosary, reclaimed in its full meaning, goes to the very heart of Christian life; it offers a familiar but fruitful spiritual and educational opportunity for personal contemplation, the formation of the People of God, and the new evangelization."

Pope John Paul II,
Rosarium Virginis Mariae, # 3

"It would be impossible to name all the saints who discovered in the Rosary a genuine path to growth in holiness. We need but mention Saint Louis Marie Grignion de Montfort, the author of an excellent work on the Rosary, and closer to ourselves, Padre Pio of Pietrelcina, whom I recently had the joy of canonizing. As a true apostle of the Rosary, Blessed Bartolo Longo had a special charism. . . . By his whole life's work . . . [he] promoted the Christocentric and contemplative heart of the Rosary."

Pope John Paul II,
Rosarium Virginis Mariae, # 8

The Joyful Mysteries

"Glory to God in the highest, and peace to God's people on earth" (Luke 2:14).

In his pastoral letter on the Rosary Pope John Paul II wrote:

The first five decades, the "joyful mysteries," are marked by the joy radiating from the event of the Incarnation. This is clear from the very first mystery, the Annunciation, where Gabriel's greeting to the Virgin of Nazareth is linked to an invitation to messianic joy: "Rejoice, Mary." The whole of salvation history, in some sense, the entire history of the world, has led up to this greeting. If it is the Father's plan to unite all things in Christ (cf. Ephesians 1:10), then the whole of the universe is in some way touched by the divine favor with which the Father looks upon Mary and makes her the Mother of his Son. The whole of humanity, in turn, is embraced by the *fiat* with which she readily agrees to the will of God.

Exultation is the keynote of the encounter with Elizabeth, where the sound of Mary's voice and the presence of Christ in her womb cause John to "leap for joy" (Luke 1:44). Gladness also fills the scene in Bethlehem, where the birth of the divine Child, the Savior of the world, is announced by the song of the angels and proclaimed to the shepherds as "news of great joy" (Luke 2:10).

The final two mysteries, while preserving this climate of joy, already point to the drama yet to come. The Presentation in the Temple not only expresses the joy of the Child's consecration and the ecstasy of the aged Simeon;

it also records the prophecy that Christ will be a "sign of contradiction" for Israel and that a sword will pierce his mother's heart (Luke 2:34–35). Joy mixed with drama marks the fifth mystery, the finding of the twelve-year-old Jesus in the Temple. Here he appears in his divine wisdom as he listens and raises questions, already in effect one who "teaches." The revelation of the mystery as the Son wholly dedicated to his Father's affairs proclaims the radical nature of the Gospel, in which even the closest of human relationships are challenged by the absolute demands of the Kingdom. Mary and Joseph, fearful and anxious, "did not understand" his words (Luke 2:50).

To meditate upon the "joyful" mysteries, then, is to enter into the ultimate causes and deepest meaning of Christian joy. It is to focus on the realism of the mystery of the Incarnation and on the obscure foreshadowing of the mystery of the sacred Passion. Mary leads us to discover the secret of

Christian joy, reminding us that Christianity is, first and foremost, *evangelion*, "good news," which has as its heart and its whole content the person of Jesus Christ, the Word made flesh, the one Savior of the world.[28]

The Holy Scriptures contain all that is needed to reveal God's full intentions for us. And yet, the life and writings of the genuine mystics in the Catholic tradition mediate the great truths of revelation for us and help us to catch the fervor of their devout lives. Love and commitment to the saving truth is their forte, and by reading them we can enter into such love and discover ways of enhancing it in our own lives.

The English mystic, Blessed Julian of Norwich (ca. 1342–1423), ranks very high among the mystics of the Western tradition. Thomas Merton called her one of the greatest theologians of all time—equal to John Henry Newman, superior to John of the Cross, and even to Teresa of Ávila.[29]

Julian represents the classic case of a mystic completely devoted to Holy Church yet able to translate its teachings and iconography into a language of description and devotion that amazes and inspires every person of faith. Here is a passage on our Lady at the time she conceived Jesus:

> God brought our Lady to my understanding. I saw her spiritually in her bodily likeness, a simple, humble maiden, young in years, of the stature which she had when she conceived. Also God showed me a part of the wisdom and truth of her soul, and in this I understood the reverent contemplation with which she held her God, marveling with great reverence that he was willing to be born of her who was a simple creature created by him. And this wisdom and truth, this knowledge of her Creator's greatness and of her own created littleness, made her say meekly to the angel Gabriel: Behold me here, God's handmaiden. In this sight I saw truly that she is greater, more worthy, and more fulfilled than anything else which God has created, and which is inferior to

her. Above her is no created thing, except the blessed humanity of Christ. This little thing [the universe] which is created and is inferior to our Lady, St. Mary—God showed it to me as if it had been a hazelnut—seemed to me as if it could have perished because it is so little.[30]

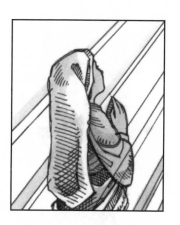

I

GABRIEL ANNOUNCES THE
GOOD NEWS TO MARY

Key Text: The angel Gabriel was sent by God to a town in Galilee called Nazareth, to a virgin engaged to a man whose name was Joseph, of the house of David. The virgin's name was Mary. And he came to her and said, "Greetings, favored one! The Lord is with you." But she was much perplexed by his words and pondered what sort of greeting this might be. The angel said to her, "Do not be afraid, Mary, for you have found favor with God. And now, you will conceive in your womb and bear a son, and you will name him Jesus. He will be great, and will be called the Son of the Most High." Then Mary said,

"Here am I, the servant of the Lord; let it be with me according to your word" (Luke 1:26–32, 38).

Other Readings: Luke 1:26–38; Isaiah 7:10–15; Matthew 1:18–25

Single Clause for Ten Hail Marys: who was conceived at the message of an angel

Ten Clauses for Ten Hail Marys:
- the Father's only Son, full of grace and truth (John 1:14)
- the reflection of God's glory and the exact imprint of God's very being (Hebrews 1:3)
- who was revealed to us at the end of the ages (1 Peter 1:20)
- whose holy name was announced to you and Joseph by angels of the Lord (Matthew 1:21 and Luke 1:31)
- whom you conceived by the overshadowing of the Holy Spirit (Luke 1:35)
- who is called great and Son of the Most High (Luke 1:32)

- who emptied himself, taking the form of a slave (Philippians 2:7)
- who was made flesh and lived among us (John 1:14)
- whose name is great among the nations (Malachi 1:11)
- whose kingdom will have no end (Luke 1:33)

Closing Prayer after the Gloria Patri

Pour forth, O Lord, your grace into our
      hearts,
that we to whom the incarnation of Christ
      your Son,
was made known by the message of an angel,
may by his passion and cross
be brought to the glory of his resurrection.
We ask this through the same Christ our
      Lord,
who lives and reigns with you and the Holy
      Spirit,
one God, for ever and ever.
~AMEN.

2
MARY VISITS HER COUSIN ELIZABETH

Key Text: In those days Mary set out and went with haste to a Judean town in the hill country, where she entered the house of Zechariah and greeted Elizabeth. When Elizabeth heard Mary's greeting, the child leaped in her womb. And Elizabeth was filled with the Holy Spirit and exclaimed with a loud cry, "Blessed are you among women, and blessed is the fruit of your womb. And why has this happened to me, that the mother of my Lord comes to me? For as soon as I heard the sound of your greeting, the child in my womb leaped for joy. And blessed is she who believed that there would be a fulfillment of what was spoken to her by the Lord." And Mary said, "My soul magnifies the Lord, and my spirit rejoices in God my Savior" (Luke 1:39–47).

Other Readings: Luke 1:39–80; Galatians 4:1–7

Single Clause: who was recognized by John the Baptist, filled with the Holy Spirit even before his birth (Luke 1:15)

Ten Clauses for Ten Hail Marys:
- the root and the descendant of David, the bright morning star (Revelation 22:16)
- who was greeted by John the Baptist from the womb of his mother Elizabeth (Luke 1:41, 44)
- who came to his people to set them free (Luke 1:68)
- who was raised up for us a mighty Savior (Luke 1:69)
- who came to save us from the hands of all who hate us (Luke 1:71)
- whose mighty arm scatters the proud in their conceit (Luke 1:51)

- who casts down the mighty from their thrones and lifts up the lowly (Luke 1:52)
- who fills the hungry with good things and sends the rich away empty (Luke 1:53)
- who shines on those who dwell in darkness and the shadow of death (Luke 1:79)
- who guides our feet into the way of peace (Luke 1:79)

Closing Prayer after the Gloria Patri

Father in heaven,
blessed is the womb that bore your only Son
and the breasts that nursed him.
When Mary entered the home of Zachary
        and Elizabeth,
their son leaped for joy in the womb
and was made holy for his prophetic mission.
By the example and intercession of these
        saints,
may we imitate their faith and devotion
and enter into everlasting joy at their side.
We ask this through Christ our Lord.
~AMEN.

3

JESUS IS BORN IN
BETHLEHEM OF JUDEA

Key Text: In that region there were shepherds living in the fields, keeping watch over their flock by night. Then an angel of the Lord stood before them, and the glory of the Lord shone around them, and they were terrified. But the angel said to them, "Do not be afraid; for see—I am bringing you good news of great joy for all the people: to you is born this day in the city of David a Savior, who is the Messiah, the Lord. This will be a sign for you: you will find a child wrapped in bands of cloth and lying in a manger." And suddenly there was with the angel a multitude of the heavenly host, praising God and saying,

"Glory to God in the highest heaven, and on earth peace among those whom he favors!" (Luke 2:8–14).

Other Readings: Luke 2:1–21; Matthew 2:1–12

Single Clause: who is good news of great joy for all the people (Luke 2:10)

Ten Clauses for Ten Hail Marys:
- the image of the God we cannot see, the firstborn of all creation (Colossians 1:15)
- the King of glory, the eternal Son of the Father (Te Deum)
- in whom all the fullness of God was pleased to dwell (Colossians 1:19)
- who is called Wonderful Counselor, Mighty God, and Prince of Peace (Isaiah 9:6)
- the Word of God made flesh for us (John 1:14)
- who was born in Bethlehem of Judea, the city of David (Luke 2:1–20)

- who is called Emmanuel, which means, "God is with us" (Matthew 1:23)
- whom God sent in the fullness of time, born of a woman, born under the law (Galatians 4:4)
- who was adored by a multitude of the heavenly host, praising God (Luke 2:13)
- who was worshipped by the shepherds of Bethlehem and the wise men from the East (Luke 2:15–20; Matthew 2:1–12)

Closing Prayer after the Gloria Patri
Father,
source of light in every age,
the Virgin conceived and bore your Son
who is called Wonderful God, Prince of
　　　　Peace.
May her prayer, the gift of a mother's love,
be your people's joy through all ages.
May her response, born of a humble heart,
draw your Spirit to rest on your people.
Grant this through Christ our Lord.
~Amen.[31]

Ten Alternate Clauses for the
Third Joyful Mystery:

- who was in the beginning with God (John 1:2)
- without whom not one thing came into being (John 1:3)
- the true light that enlightens everyone (John 1:9)
- who came to what was his own and his own people did not accept him (John 1:11)
- who gave us power to become children of God (John 1:12)
- the Word of God who became flesh and lived among us (John 1:14)
- the glory of the Father's only Son, full of grace and truth (John 1:14)
- from whose fullness we have all received, grace upon grace (John 1:16)
- God the only Son, close to the Father's heart, who has made him known (John 1:18)
- the Lamb of God who takes away the sin of the world (John 1:29)

Closing Prayer after the Gloria Patri
Lord Christ,
to celebrate your coming among us,
you selected servants to reveal yourself to us:
from among the angels, the Archangel
            Gabriel;
from the human race, the Blessed Virgin
            Mary;
from the heavens, a guiding star;
from the prophets, John the Baptizer;
from earth's waters, the Jordan,
by which you washed away our sins
and made us children of the Most High.
Glory to you, O Lord.
~AMEN.

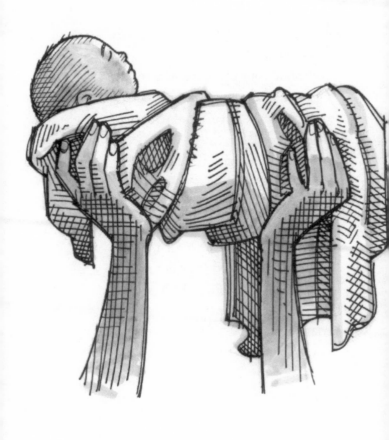

4

MARY AND JOSEPH PRESENT
JESUS IN THE TEMPLE

Key Text: When the time came for their puri-
fication according to the law of Moses, they
brought him up to Jerusalem to present him to
the Lord, and they offered a sacrifice according to what is stated in the law of the Lord, "a
pair of turtledoves or two young pigeons." Now
there was a man in Jerusalem whose name was
Simeon; this man was righteous and devout,
looking forward to the consolation of Israel,
and the Holy Spirit rested on him. It had
been revealed to him by the Holy Spirit that
he would not see death before he had seen the
Lord's Messiah. Guided by the Spirit, Simeon
came into the temple; and when the parents

brought in the child Jesus, to do for him what was customary under the law, Simeon took him in his arms and praised God (Luke 2:22–28).

Other Readings: Luke 2:22–40; Leviticus 12:1–8; Exodus 13:1–2, 11–12; Malachi 3:1–4

Single Clause: a light of revelation to the nations and the glory of your people Israel (Luke 2:32)

Ten Clauses for Ten Hail Marys:
• God's true and only Son, worthy of all praise (Te Deum)
• who humbly chose your virgin womb (Te Deum)
• who came to fulfill the Law of Moses (Luke 2:22–24)
• who suddenly came to the Temple of the Lord (Malachi 3:1)
• whom you and Joseph presented in the Temple (Luke 2:22–40)

- who was recognized as Israel's Messiah by old Simeon and Anna (Luke 2:27–38)
- a light of revelation to the nations and the glory of your people Israel (Luke 2:32)
- a child destined for the falling and rising of many in Israel (Luke 2:34)
- a sign that will be opposed and a sword of division (Luke 2:34)
- who allowed a sword to pierce your own soul too (Luke 2:35)

Closing Prayer after the Gloria Patri
Almighty and merciful God,
old Simeon and Anna rejoiced
as Mary and Joseph presented your Son
in the temple of Jerusalem.
May we enter into their joy as he reveals
        himself
as a light of revelation to the nations
and await his coming in glory at the end
        of time.
We ask this through the same Christ our Lord.
~Amen.

5
MARY AND JOSEPH FIND JESUS IN THE TEMPLE

Key Text: Now every year Jesus' parents went to Jerusalem for the festival of the Passover. And when he was twelve years old, they went up as usual to the festival. When the festival was ended and they started to return, the boy Jesus stayed behind in Jerusalem, but his parents did not know it. When they did not find him, they returned to Jerusalem to search for him. After three days they found him in the temple, sitting among the teachers, listening to them and asking them questions. And all who heard him were amazed at his understanding and his answers. When his parents saw him they were astonished; and his mother said to him, "Child, why have you treated us like this? Look, your father and I have been searching for you in great anxiety." He said to them, "Why were you searching for me? Did you not know that I must be in my Father's house?" Then he went down with them and came to Nazareth, and was obedient to them. His mother treasured all these things in her heart (Luke 2:41–43, 45–49, 51).

Other Readings: Exodus 23:14–15; Deuteronomy 16:1–8

Single Clause: the power of God and the wisdom of God (1 Corinthians 1:24)

Ten Clauses for Ten Hail Marys:
- whose word is a lamp for our feet and a light for our path (Psalm 119:105)
- who, when he was twelve years old, went with you and Joseph to celebrate the Passover at Jerusalem (Luke 2:41–42)

- who stayed behind in his Father's house when his parents left the city (Luke 2:43)
- for whom you and Joseph searched with great anxiety (Luke 2:44–45)
- whom you found sitting among the teachers in the temple, listening to them and asking them questions (Luke 2:46)
- who amazed them all by his understanding and his answers (Luke 2:47)
- who knew he had to be in his Father's house and about his Father's business (Luke 2:49)
- who obediently returned to Nazareth with you and Joseph (Luke 2:51)
- who moved you to treasure all these things in your heart (Luke 2:51)
- who grew in wisdom and in years, and in divine and human favor (Luke 2:52)

Closing Prayer after the Gloria Patri
Lord God of Israel,
source of light in every age,

you revealed to Mary and Joseph
the true calling of their only Son
when they found him again in the temple.
By his intelligence and wisdom,
make us marvel at his understanding
and come to revere in all its fullness
the dual nature of the Word made flesh.
We ask this through the same Christ our
        Lord.
~Amen.

After the Joyous Mysteries: *Alma Redemptoris Mater*

Mother of Christ, our hope, our patroness,
~Star of the sea, our beacon in
        distress,
Guide to the shores of everlasting day
God's holy people on their pilgrim way.

Virgin, in you God made his dwelling
        place;
Mother of all the living, full of
        grace,

BLESSED ARE YOU: GOD'S WORD YOU DID
  BELIEVE;
"YES" ON YOUR LIPS UNDID THE "NO" OF EVE.

DAUGHTER OF GOD, WHO BORE HIS HOLY
  ONE,
DEAREST OF ALL TO CHRIST, YOUR LOVING
  SON,
SHOW US HIS FACE, O MOTHER, AS ON
  EARTH,
LOVING US ALL, YOU GAVE OUR SAVIOR
  BIRTH.[32]

The Word was made flesh, alleluia!
~AND LIVED AMONG US, ALLELUIA!

Let us pray:

Father of Jesus,
by the fruitful virginity of Mary
you conferred salvation on the whole human
  race.
May we experience her intercession for us

through whom we have received the Author
of life,
our Lord Jesus Christ, your Son,
who lives and reigns with you and the Holy
Spirit,
one God, for ever and ever.
~Amen.

Blessing
May the Virgin Mother mild
† bless us with her holy child.
~Amen

The Luminous Mysteries

"This is my Son, the Beloved; listen to him!"
(Mark 9:7).

In his pastoral letter on the Rosary, Pope John Paul
II wrote:

> Moving on from the infancy and the hid-
> den life in Nazareth to the public life of
> Jesus, our contemplation brings us to those
> mysteries which may be called in a spe-
> cial way "mysteries of light." Certainly the
> whole mystery of Christ is a mystery of
> light. He is the "light of the world" (John
> 8:12). Yet this truth emerges in a special

way during the years of his public life, when he proclaims the Gospel of the Kingdom. In proposing to the Christian community five significant moments—"luminous" mysteries—during this phase of Christ's life, I think that the following can be fittingly singled out: 1) his Baptism in the Jordan, 2) his self-manifestation at the wedding of Cana, 3) his proclamation of the Kingdom of God, with his call to conversion, 4) his Transfiguration, and finally, 5) his institution of the Eucharist, as the sacramental expression of the Paschal Mystery.

Each of these mysteries is *a revelation of the Kingdom now present in the very person of Jesus.* The Baptism in the Jordan is first of all a mystery of light. Here, as Christ descends into the waters, the innocent who became "sin" for our sake (cf. 2 Corinthians 5:21), the heavens open wide and the voice of the Father declares him the beloved Son (Mark 3:17 and parallels), while the Spirit descends on him to invest him with the mission which he is to carry out. Another mystery of light is the first of the signs, given at Cana (John 2:1–12), when Christ changes water into wine and opens the hearts of the disciples to faith, thanks to the intervention of Mary, the first among believers. Another mystery of light is the preaching by which Jesus proclaims the coming of the Kingdom of God, calls us to conversion (Mark 1:15), and forgives the sins of all who draw near to him in humble trust (cf. Mark 2:3–13; Luke 7:47–48): the inauguration of that ministry of mercy which he continues to exercise until the end of the world, particularly through the Sacrament of Reconciliation which he has entrusted to his Church (John 20:22–23).

The mystery of light par excellence is the Transfiguration, traditionally believed to have taken place on Mount Tabor [Northern Galilee]. The glory of the Godhead shines forth from the face of Christ as the Father commands the astonished Apostles to "listen to him" (Luke 9:35 and parallels) and to prepare to experience with him the agony of the Passion, so as to come with him to the joy of the Resurrection and a life transformed by the Holy Spirit. A final mystery of light is the institution of the Eucharist, in which Christ offers his body and blood as food under the signs of bread and wine, and testifies "to the end" his love for humanity (John 13:1), for whose salvation he will offer himself in sacrifice.

In these mysteries, apart from the miracle of Cana, *the presence of Mary remains in the background.* The Gospels only make the briefest reference to her occasional presence at one moment or other during the preaching of Jesus (cf. Mark 3:31–35; John 2:12). . . . Yet the role she assumed at Cana in some way accompanies Christ throughout his ministry. The revelation made directly by the Father at the Baptism in the Jordan and echoed by John the Baptist is placed upon

Mary's lips at Cana, and it becomes the great maternal counsel which Mary addresses to the Church of every age: "Do whatever he tells you" (John 2:5). This counsel is a fitting introduction to the words and signs of Christ's public ministry and it forms the Marian foundation of all the mysteries of light.[33]

Let us return again to Blessed Julian of Norwich:

Our Lord gave special understanding and teaching about the working and revelation of miracles, thus: It is known that I have performed miracles in time past, many, most great and wonderful, glorious and splendid, and what I have done I always go on doing, and I shall in time to come. It is known that before miracles come sorrows and anguish and trouble, and that because we ought to know our own weakness, and the harm that we have fallen into through sin, to humble us and make us cry to God for help and grace.

And afterwards great miracles come, and that is from God's great power and wisdom and goodness, showing his might and the joys of heaven, as much as this may be in this passing life, and that is for the strengthening of our faith, and as this may increase our hope in love. Therefore it pleases him to be known and worshipped in miracles. Then this is his intention: He wishes us not to be oppressed because of the sorrows and travails which come to us, for it has always been so before the coming of miracles.[34]

I

JESUS IS BAPTIZED BY
JOHN IN THE JORDAN

Key Text: Jesus came from Nazareth of Galilee and was baptized by John in the Jordan. And just as he was coming up out of the water, he saw the heavens torn apart and the Spirit descending like a dove on him. And a voice came from heaven, "You are my Son, the Beloved; with you I am well pleased." And the Spirit immediately drove him out into the wilderness. He was in the wilderness forty days, tempted by Satan; and he was with the wild beasts; and the angels waited on him (Mark 1:9–13).

Other Readings: Matthew 3:13–17; Luke 3:15–22; John 1:29–34

Single Clause for Ten Hail Marys: the beloved Son of God in whom the Father is well pleased (Mark 1:11)

Ten Clauses for Ten Hail Marys:
- who came from Nazareth of Galilee and was baptized by John in the Jordan (Mark 1:9)
- on whom the Spirit of God descended like a dove (Mark 1:10)
- the beloved Son of God in whom the Father is well pleased (Mark 1:11)
- the Lamb of God who takes away the sin of the world (John 1:36)
- the one who baptizes with the Holy Spirit and with fire (Matthew 3:11)
- who cleansed and sanctified the waters for our baptism
- who was driven into the wilderness by the Spirit (Mark 1:12)
- who fasted for forty days and nights in the wilderness and was tempted by Satan (Mark 1:13; Luke 4:1–2)

- who was with the wild beasts and waited on by angels (Mark 1:13)
- who after John was arrested came into Galilee, proclaiming the good news of God (Mark 1:14)

Closing Prayer after the Gloria Patri
Almighty, eternal God,
when the Spirit descended upon Jesus
at his baptism in the Jordan,
you revealed him as your own beloved Son.
Keep us, your children, born of water and the Spirit,
faithful to our Christian calling.
We ask this through Christ our Lord.
~Amen.[35]

2

JESUS AND MARY ATTEND THE
WEDDING FEAST OF CANA

Key Text: There was a wedding in Cana of Galilee, and the mother of Jesus was there. Jesus and his disciples had also been invited to the wedding. When the wine gave out, the mother of Jesus said to him, "They have no wine." And Jesus said to her, "Woman, what concern is that to you and to me? My hour has not yet come." His mother said to the servants, "Do whatever he tells you." Jesus said to them, "Fill the jars with water." And they filled them up to the brim. He said to them, "Now draw some out, and take it to the chief steward." So they took it. When the steward tasted the water that had become wine, . . . the steward called the bridegroom and said to him, "Everyone serves the good wine first, and then the inferior wine after the guests have become drunk. But you have kept the good wine until now." Jesus did this, the first of his signs, in Cana of Galilee, and revealed his glory; and his disciples believed in him. After this he went down to Capernaum with his mother, his brothers, and his disciples (John 2:1–5, 7–12).

Single Clause: who revealed his glory at the wedding at Cana (John 2:11)

Ten Clauses for Ten Hail Marys:
- who was invited to a wedding at Cana of Galilee with you and his first disciples (John 2:1–2)
- who listened to your request as the wine gave out (John 2:3)
- who told you his hour had not yet come (John 2:4)
- who told the servants to fill the six stone jars with water (John 2:6–7)
- who changed the water into wine at your request (John 2:5)

- who gladdened the guests by water made wine (John 2:9–10)
- who did this, the first of his signs, in Cana of Galilee (John 2:11)
- who revealed his glory; and his disciples believed in him (John 2:11)
- who changed the water of the Old Covenant into the wine of the New
- who glorified you as the new Eve and the mother of all the living

Closing Prayer after the Gloria Patri
Lord and Savior,
you listened to your mother at Cana
and lavished your care on the wedding party
by changing water into wine for them.
By the loving intercession of Mary,
the first among believers,
come to our assistance in time of need
and help us read the signs of your presence
in our lives.
May you reign in the hearts of your people,
now and for ever.
~Amen.

3

JESUS PREACHES AND INAUGURATES THE IMMINENT REIGN OF GOD

Key Text: Now after John was arrested, Jesus came to Galilee, proclaiming the good news of God, and saying, "The time is fulfilled, and the kingdom of God has come near; repent, and believe in the good news" (Mark 1:14–15).

When John heard in prison what the Messiah was doing, he sent word by his disciples and said to Jesus, "Are you the one who is to come, or are we to wait for another?" Jesus answered them, "Go and tell John what you hear and see: the blind receive their sight, the lame walk, the lepers are cleansed, the deaf hear, the dead are raised, and the poor have good news brought to them. And blessed is anyone who takes no offense at me" (Matthew 11:2–6).

Jesus went throughout Galilee, teaching in their synagogues and proclaiming the good news of the kingdom and curing every disease and every sickness among the people. So his fame spread throughout all Syria, and they brought to him all the sick, those who were afflicted with various diseases and pains, demoniacs, epileptics, and paralytics, and he cured them. And great crowds followed him from Galilee, the Decapolis, Jerusalem, Judea, and from beyond the Jordan (Matthew 4:23–25).

Other Readings: Matthew 4:12–25, 9:35, 15:29–31; Mark 1:29–34; Luke 4:14–21

Single Clause: who proclaimed the coming reign of God (Mark 1:15)

Ten Clauses for Ten Hail Marys:

- who, filled with the power of the Spirit, returned to Galilee (Luke 4:14)
- who left Nazareth and made his home in Capernaum by the sea (Matthew 4:13)
- who began to teach in their synagogues and was praised by everyone (Luke 4:15)
- who proclaimed, "Repent, for the kingdom of heaven has come near" (Matthew 4:17)
- who went about doing good, healing every manner of sickness and disease (Matthew 15:29–31)
- who taught as one having authority and not as the scribes (Mark 1:22)
- who cast out unclean spirits and raised Lazarus from the grave (Mark 1:32–34, 39; John 11:1–44)
- who was followed by great crowds from Galilee, Judea, and from beyond the Jordan (Matthew 4:25)
- who taught the crowds from the Mount of the Beatitudes (Matthew 5:1–2)

• who came to fulfill the law and the
  prophets (Matthew 5:17)

Closing Prayer after the Gloria Patri
Lord Jesus, Holy One of God,
during your public ministry
you went about doing good
and proclaiming the imminent reign of God.
Confident in your authority and your
        goodness,
we beg you to cast out our demons,
cure our diseases and afflictions,
and make us responsive to the word of God.
You live and reign with the Father and the
        Holy Spirit,
now and for ever.
~Amen.

4

Jesus Is Transfigured on Mount Tabor

Key Text: Jesus took with him Peter and James and John, and led them up a high mountain apart, by themselves. And he was transfigured before them, and his clothes became dazzling white, such as no one on earth could bleach them. And there appeared to them Elijah with Moses, who were talking with Jesus. Then a cloud overshadowed them, and from the cloud there came a voice, "This is my Son, the Beloved; listen to him!" (Mark 9:2–4, 7).

Other Readings: Mark 9:2–13; Matthew 17:1–9; Luke 9:28–36; 2 Peter 1:16–18

Single Clause: whose face shone like the sun and whose clothes became dazzling white (Matthew 17:2)

Ten Clauses for Ten Hail Marys:
- who is the refulgence of God's glory, the very imprint of God's being (Hebrews 1:3, NAB)
- who took Peter, James, and John to pray with him on Mount Tabor (Luke 9:28)
- who during the night was transfigured before them on the holy mountain (Matthew 17:2; Luke 9:32)
- whose face shone like the sun and whose clothes became dazzling white (Matthew 17:2)
- who made his disciples eyewitnesses of his majesty (2 Peter 1:16)
- with whom Moses and Elijah appeared in glory, and spoke of his coming exodus at Jerusalem (Luke 9:31)
- whose terrified disciples were overshadowed by a bright cloud (Luke 9:34)

- God's chosen and beloved Son to whom we must listen (Mark 9:7; Luke 9:35)
- who ordered them to tell no one about what they had seen until after he was raised from the dead (Matthew 17:9)
- who will transform our humble bodies and make them like his own glorious body (Philippians 3:21)

Closing Prayer after the Gloria Patri
Heavenly Father,
in the transfigured glory of Jesus,
you confirmed the witness of your prophets,
revealed the splendor of the Word made flesh,
and prepared the disciples for his coming death.
As we listen to the voice of your dear Son,
show us as much of his glory as we can stand,
teach us the beautiful truths of the Gospel,
and make us heirs to eternal life with him,
who lives and reigns with you,
in the unity of the Holy Spirit,
one God, for ever and ever.
~Amen.

5
JESUS INSTITUTES
THE LORD'S SUPPER

Key Text: I received from the Lord what I also handed on to you, that the Lord Jesus on the night when he was betrayed took a loaf of bread, and when he had given thanks, he broke it and said, "This is my body that is for you. Do this in remembrance of me." In the same way he took the cup also, after supper, saying, "This cup is the new covenant in my blood. Do this, as often as you drink it, in remembrance of me." For as often as you eat this bread and drink the cup, you proclaim the Lord's death until he comes (1 Corinthians 11:23–26).

Other Readings: Matthew 26:26–30; Mark 12:22–25; Luke 22:15–20; John 6:25–71

Single Clause: whose flesh is true food and whose blood is true drink (John 6:55)

Ten Clauses for Ten Hail Marys:
- the high priest and mediator of the new and eternal covenant (Hebrews 9:11)
- who eagerly desired to eat the Passover with his disciples before he suffered (Luke 22:15)
- who humbly washed the feet of his disciples at the last supper (John 13:5)
- who provided us with a living memorial of his passion (Luke 22:19)
- who gives us the living bread from heaven to eat (John 6:33)
- who gives us the food that endures for eternal life (John 6:27)
- who gives us his blood of the covenant, which is poured out for the forgiveness of sins (Matthew 26:28)

- whose flesh is true food and whose blood is true drink (John 6:55)
- the Holy One of God who has the words of eternal life (John 6:68–69)
- who will raise us up on the last day (John 6:39)

Closing Prayer after the Gloria Patri
Lord Jesus Christ,
we worship you living among us
in the sacrament of your body and blood.
May we offer to our Father in heaven
a solemn pledge of undivided love.
May we offer to our brothers and sisters
a life poured out in loving service of that
        kingdom
where you live with the Father,
in the unity of the Holy Spirit,
one God, for ever and ever.
~AMEN.[36]

After the Mysteries of Light: *Sub Tuum Praesidium*
We turn to you for protection,
~HOLY MOTHER OF GOD.
LISTEN TO OUR PRAYERS
AND HELP US IN OUR NEEDS.
SAVE US FROM EVERY DANGER,
GLORIOUS AND BLESSED VIRGIN.[37]

Pray for us, holy Mother of God,
~THAT WE MAY BECOME WORTHY
OF THE PROMISES OF CHRIST.

Let us pray:

Eternal Father,
you have established in the Virgin Mary
the royal throne of your wisdom.
Enlighten the Church by the Word of life,
that we may walk in the splendor of truth

and come to the full knowledge
    of your mystery of love.
We ask this through Christ our Lord.
~AMEN.[38]

Blessing
May the Word made flesh, the Son of Mary,
† bless us and keep us.
~AMEN.

The Sorrowful Mysteries

"See, we are going up to Jerusalem, and the Son of Man will be handed over to the chief priests and the scribes, and they will condemn him to death; then they will hand him over to the Gentiles; they will mock him, and spit upon him, and flog him, and kill him; and after three days he will rise again" (Mark 10:33–34).

In his pastoral letter on the Rosary, Pope John Paul II wrote:

The Gospels give great prominence to the sorrowful mysteries of Christ. From the beginning Christian piety, especially during the Lenten devotion of the *Way of the Cross*, has focused on the individual moments of the Passion, realizing that here is found the *culmination of the revelation of God's love* and the source of our salvation. The Rosary selects certain moments of the Passion, inviting the faithful to contemplate them in their hearts and to relive them. The sequence of meditations begins with Gethsemane, where Christ experiences a moment of great anguish before the will of the Father, against which the weakness of the flesh would be tempted to rebel. There Jesus encounters all the temptations and confronts all the sins of humanity, in order to say to the Father: "Not my will but yours be done" (Luke 22:42 and parallels). This "Yes" of Christ reverses the "No" of our first parents in the Garden of Eden. And the cost of this faithfulness to the Father's will is made clear in the following mysteries; by his scourging, his crowning with thorns, his carrying the Cross, and his death on the Cross, the Lord is cast into the most abject suffering: *Ecce homo!*

This abject suffering reveals not only the love of God but also the meaning of man himself. *Ecce homo:* the meaning, origin and fulfillment of man is to be found in Christ, the God who humbles himself out of love "even to death, death on a cross" (Philippians 2:8). The sorrowful mysteries help the believer to relive the death of Jesus, to stand at the foot of the Cross beside Mary, to enter with her into the depths of God's love and to experience all its life-giving power.[39]

Devout believer that she was, Julian of Norwich longed to experience Jesus' passion and death more fully. At age thirty and a half she was granted the extraordinary favor (May 13, 1373) of a series of sixteen "showings" of Jesus undergoing his bitter passion, cruel death, and glorious resurrection.

Like many of Christ's friends, Julian "had great
feeling for the Passion of Christ," but still she
desired more.

> I thought that I wished that I had been at
> the time with Mary Magdalen and with the
> others who were Christ's lovers, so that I
> might have seen with my own eyes our Lord's
> Passion which he suffered for me, so that I
> might have suffered with him as others who
> loved him, even though I firmly believed in
> all Christ's pains, as Holy Church shows and
> teaches, and as paintings of the Crucifixion
> represent, which are made by God's grace,
> according to Holy Church's teaching, to
> resemble Christ's Passion, so far as human
> understanding can attain. But despite all my
> true faith, I desired a bodily sight through
> which I might have more knowledge of our
> Lord and Saviour's bodily pains, and of the
> compassion of our Lady and of all his true
> lovers for I would have been one of them and
> have suffered with them. . . .

With a kindly countenance our good Lord looked into his side, and he gazed with joy, and with his sweet regard he drew his creature's understanding into his side by the same wound; and there he revealed a fair and delectable place, large enough for all mankind that will be saved and will rest in peace and in love. And with that he brought to mind the dear and precious blood and water which he suffered to be shed for love. And in this sweet sight he showed his blessed heart split in two, and as she rejoiced he showed to my understanding a part of his blessed divinity, as much as was his will at that time, strengthening my poor soul to understand what can be said, that is the endless love which was without beginning and is and always shall be.

And with this our good Lord said most joyfully: See how I love you, as if he had said, my darling, behold and see your Lord, your God, who is your Creator and your endless joy; see your own brother, your saviour; my child, behold and see what delight and bliss I have in your salvation, and for my love rejoice with me.

And for my great understanding, these blessed words were said: See how I love you, as if he had said, behold and see that I loved you so much, before I died for you, that I wanted to die for you. And now I have died for you, and willingly suffered what I could. And now all my bitter pain and hard labour is turned into everlasting joy and bliss for me and for you. How could it now be that you would pray to me for anything pleasing to me which I would not very gladly grant to you? For my delight is in your holiness and in your endless joy and bliss in me.[40]

I

The Agony of Jesus in the Garden of Gethsemane

Key Text: When they had sung the hymn [Psalms 115–118, at the end of the Passover meal], they went out to the Mount of Olives to a place called Gethsemane; and he said to his disciples, "Sit here while I go over there and pray." He took with him Peter and the two sons of Zebedee, and began to be grieved and agitated. Then he said to them, "I am deeply grieved, even to death; remain here, and stay awake with me." And going a little farther, he threw himself on the ground and prayed, "My Father, if it is possible, let this cup pass from me; yet not what I want but what you want."

Then he came to the disciples and found them sleeping; and he said to Peter, "So, could you not stay awake with me one hour? Stay awake and pray that you may not come into the time of trial; the spirit indeed is willing, but the flesh is weak." Again he went away for the second time and prayed, "My Father, if this cannot pass unless I drink it, your will be done." Again he came and found them sleeping, for their eyes were heavy. So leaving them again, he went away and prayed for the third time, saying the same words. Then he came to the disciples and said to them, "Are you still sleeping and taking your rest? See, the hour is at hand, and the Son of Man is betrayed into the hands of sinners. Get up, let us be going. See, my betrayer is at hand" (Matthew 26:30, 36–46).

Other Readings: Mark 14:32–50; Luke 22:40–46; John 12:27–36; John 18:1–14; Hebrews 5:7–10

Single Clause for Ten Hail Marys: who was betrayed into the hands of sinners (Matthew 26:45; Mark 14:41)

Ten Clauses for Ten Hail Marys:

- who knew that his hour had come to go to the Father (John 13:1)
- who went out to the Mount of Olives to pray with his disciples (Mark 14:26)
- who asked his disciples to keep watch with him in the garden of Gethsemane (Mark 14:32–42)
- who prayed in great agony and distress to his Father (Mark 14:33)
- whose sweat became like great drops of blood falling to the ground (Luke 22:44)
- who was deeply grieved even to death (Matthew 26:38)
- who came to his disciples three times and found them sleeping (Matthew 26:40)
- who was betrayed by Judas with a kiss and deserted by all his disciples (Mark 14:45)

- who was arrested, bound, and taken to
  Caiaphas, the high priest (Mark 14:53–65)
- who was denied three times by Peter before
  cockcrow (Mark 14:53–54, 66–72)

Closing Prayer after the Gloria Patri
Lord Jesus, man of sorrows,
by your prolonged agony in the garden,
blot out our sins of sloth and apathy
and keep us awake in your presence.
May we never betray you with Judas,
desert you with your chosen friends,
or deny you with Simon Peter,
but accompany you in faith and hope
on the long road to Calvary.
You live and reign with the Father and the
        Holy Spirit,
now and for ever.
~Amen.

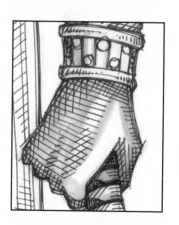

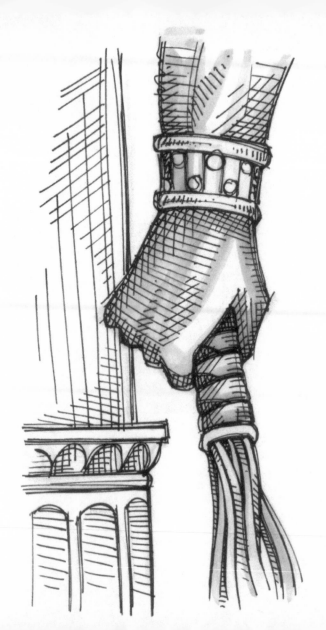

2

JESUS IS TRIED, CONDEMNED, AND FLOGGED BY PILATE

Key Text: As soon as it was morning, the chief priests held a consultation with the elders and scribes and the whole council. They bound Jesus, led him away, and handed him over to Pilate. Pilate asked him, "Are you the King of the Jews?" He answered him, "You say so." Then the chief priests accused him of many things. Pilate asked him again, "Have you no answer? See how many charges they bring against you." But Jesus made no further reply, so that Pilate was amazed.

Now at the festival [Passover] Pilate used to release a prisoner for them, anyone for whom they asked. Now a man called Barabbas was in prison with the rebels who had committed murder during the insurrection. So the crowd came and began to ask Pilate to do for them according to his custom. Then he answered them, "Do you want me to release for you the King of the Jews?" For he realized that it was out of jealousy that the chief priests had handed him over. But the chief priests stirred up the crowd to have him release Barabbas for them instead. Pilate spoke to them again, "Then what do you wish me to do with the man you call the King of the Jews?" They shouted back, "Crucify him!" Pilate asked them, "Why, what evil has he done?" But they shouted all the more, "Crucify him!" So Pilate, wishing to satisfy the crowd, released Barabbas for them; and after flogging Jesus, he handed him over to be crucified (Mark 15:1–15).

Other Readings: Matthew 27:1–2, 11–26; Luke 23:1–25; John 18:28–19:1

Single Clause: who was flogged and handed over to be crucified (Mark 15:15)

Ten Clauses for Ten Hail Marys:
- who was tried and condemned by the high priest for blasphemy (Mark 14:64)
- who was blindfolded, spat upon, and beaten by the guards (Mark 14:65)
- who was put in chains and handed over to Pilate the governor (Mark 15:1)
- who kept silence in the face of his accusers (Mark 15:2–5)
- whom Pilate traded for Barabbas, a notorious bandit and murderer (Mark 15:7)
- who was sentenced to die a shameful death on the cross (Wisdom 2:20)
- who was handed over to be flogged like a slave (Mark 15:15)
- who gave his back to those who struck him (Isaiah 50:6)
- who was wounded for our transgressions and crushed for our iniquities (Isaiah 53:5)

• by whose wounds we are healed
  (Isaiah 53:5)

Closing Prayer after the Gloria Patri
Jesus, suffering servant of God,
cruelly betrayed by Judas for money,
condemned for blasphemy by Caiaphas,
unjustly sentenced to death by Pontius Pilate:
By your bitter passion and the compassion
of your sorrowing Mother,
fix your suffering and death in our hearts
and make us faithful disciples of the Gospel
     of truth,
now and for ever.
~Amen.

3
Jesus Is Treated as a Mock King and Crowned with Thorns

Key Text: Then the soldiers led him into the courtyard of the palace . . . ; and they called together the whole cohort. And they clothed him in a purple cloak; and after twisting some thorns into a crown, they put it on him. And they began saluting him, "Hail, King of the Jews!" They struck his head with a reed, spat upon him, and knelt down in homage to him. After mocking him, they stripped him of his purple cloak and put his own clothes on him. Then they led him out to crucify him (Mark 15:16–20).

Other Readings: Matthew 27:27–31; John 19:1–7

Single Clause: who was crowned with thorns and mocked as King of the Jews (Mark 15:17–18)

Ten Clauses for Ten Hail Marys:
- a man of suffering and acquainted with infirmity (Isaiah 53:3)
- who was despised and rejected and held of no account (Isaiah 53:3)
- who was surrounded by the whole cohort of brutal soldiers (Mark 15:16)
- who was stripped of his clothes and dressed in a purple robe of mockery (Matthew 27:28; Mark 15:17)
- whose head was crowned with piercing thorns (Mark 15:17)
- who was struck in the face, spat upon, and mocked as King of the Jews (Mark 15:19; John 19:3)

- who was crushed with pain for us
  (Isaiah 53:10)
- whom Pilate handed over to be crucified
  (Mark 15:15)
- who was like a lamb led to the slaughter
  (Isaiah 53:7)
- the righteous one who shall make many
  righteous (Isaiah 53:11)

Closing Prayer after the Gloria Patri
Jesus, suffering servant of God,
after your brutal flogging
you were exposed to mockery and derision
and hailed as King of the Jews
by a cohort of pitiless soldiers.
Be with us when we are excluded,
mocked, and humiliated for your sake,
and inspire us by your courageous silence
and undying witness to the truth,
O Savior of the world,
living and reigning, now and for ever.
~Amen.

4

JESUS WALKS THE
WAY OF THE CROSS

Key Text: As they led him away, they seized a man, Simon of Cyrene, who was coming from the country, and they laid the cross on him, and made him carry it behind Jesus. A great number of the people followed him, and among them were women who were beating their breasts and wailing for him. But Jesus turned to them and said, "Daughters of Jerusalem, do not weep for me, but weep for yourselves and for your children. For the days are surely coming when they will say, 'Blessed are the barren, and the wombs that never bore, and the breasts that never nursed.' Then they will begin to say to the mountains, 'Fall on us'; and to the hills, 'Cover us.' For if they do this when the wood is green, what will happen when it is dry?" (Luke 23:26–31).

Other Readings: Isaiah 53:1–5; Matthew 27:32–37; Mark 15:21–24; John 19:16–25

Single Clause: who went out to the Place of a Skull carrying the cross by himself (John 19:17)

Ten Clauses for Ten Hail Marys:
- who was led out to be crucified and tested with insult and torture (Mark 15:20; Wisdom 2:19)
- who went out to Golgotha carrying the cross by himself (John 19:17)
- who was led away with two criminals to be put to death (Mark 15:32; Luke 23:32)
- who was assisted by Simon of Cyrene, who was made to carry the cross behind him (Mark 15:21)
- who was followed by a crowd of women beating their breasts and wailing for him (Luke 23:27)

- who said to the women, "Do not weep for me, but for yourselves and for your children" (Luke 23:28)
- who, when he arrived at Golgotha, was offered wine mixed with myrrh; but he did not take it (Mark 15:23)
- who was stripped of his clothes and nailed to the cross (Mark 15:24)
- the Good Shepherd, who was willing to lay down his life for the sheep (John 10:11)
- whose cross will appear in the heavens when he returns with power and great glory (Matthew 24:30)

Closing Prayer after the Gloria Patri
Abba, dear Father,
look upon this family of yours
for which our Lord Jesus Christ
did not hesitate to hand himself over to sinners
and to undergo the torment of the cross.
He lives and reigns with you,
in the unity of the Holy Spirit,
one God, for ever and ever.
~AMEN.

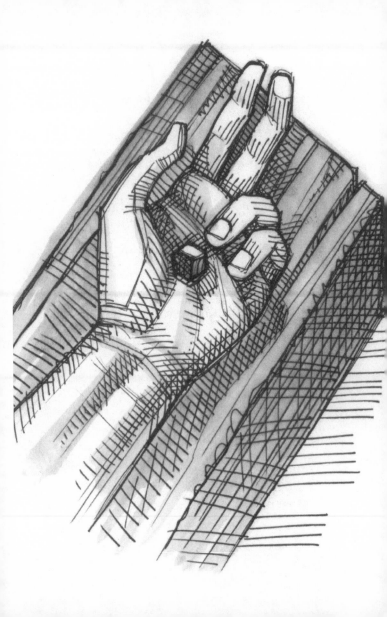

5
JESUS IS CRUCIFIED, DIES ON THE CROSS, AND IS BURIED

Key Text: It was nine o'clock in the morning when they crucified him. The inscription of the charge against him read, "The King of the Jews." And with him they crucified two bandits, one on his right and one on his left. Those who passed by derided him, shaking their heads and saying, "Aha! You who would destroy the temple and build it in three days, save yourself, and come down from the cross!" Those who were crucified with him also taunted him. When it was noon, darkness came over the whole land until three in the afternoon. At three o'clock Jesus cried out with a loud voice, "My God, my God, why have you forsaken me?" (Mark 15:25–30, 32–34).

Meanwhile, standing near the cross of Jesus were his mother, and his mother's sister, Mary the wife of Clopas, and Mary Magdalene. When Jesus saw his mother and the disciple whom he loved standing beside her, he said to his mother, "Woman, here is your son." Then he said to the disciple, "Here is your mother." And from that hour the disciple took her into his own home (John 19:25–27).

After this, when Jesus knew that all was now finished, he said (in order to fulfill the scripture), "I am thirsty." A jar full of sour wine was standing there. So they put a sponge full of the wine on a branch of hyssop and held it to his mouth. When Jesus had received the wine, he said, "It is finished." Then he bowed his head and gave up his spirit (John 19:28–30).

Other Readings: Matthew 27:32–61; Luke 23:26–56; John 19:1–42

Single Clause: whose blood is poured out for us for the forgiveness of sins (Matthew 26:28; Mark 14:24)

Ten Clauses for Ten Hail Marys:
- who humbled himself to the point of death—even death on the cross (Philippians 2:8)
- who held out his hands all day long to a disobedient and contrary people (Isaiah 65:2; Romans 10:21)
- who was wounded for our transgressions and crushed for our sins (Isaiah 53:5)
- who was derided by those who passed by, scoffed at by priests, and taunted by those who were crucified with him (Mark 15:25–32)
- who from the cross forgave his enemies and promised Paradise to a repentant criminal (Luke 23:34, 43)
- who from the cross entrusted you, mother of sorrows, to his beloved disciple (John 19:25–27)

- who, at three o'clock, gave a loud cry and breathed his last (Mark 15:37)
- whose sacred heart was pierced by a Roman spear and poured out blood and water (John 19:33–34)
- whose body noble Joseph wrapped in a linen shroud and laid in his rock-hewn tomb (Mark 15:46)
- who went down among the dead to bring them the Good News (1 Peter 3:19; 4:6)

Closing Prayer after the Gloria Patri

Lord Jesus Christ, Son of the living God,
set your passion, your cross, and your death
between your judgment and our souls,
now and at the hour of our death.
In your great goodness,
grant mercy and grace to the living
and forgiveness and rest to the dead;
to the church and to the nations peace and
        concord;
and to us sinners life and glory without end.
~AMEN.[41]

Ten Alternate Clauses for the Fifth Sorrowful Mystery:

- who was crucified between two criminals (Matthew 27:38)
- whose clothes were divided among the soldiers by casting lots (Matthew 27:35)
- who was derided by those who passed by (Matthew 27:39)
- who was mocked by the chief priests, the scribes, and the elders of the people (Matthew 27:39–43)
- who was taunted by the bandits who were crucified with him (Matthew 27:44)
- for whom darkness came over the whole land until three in the afternoon (Matthew 27:45)
- who, at about three o'clock, cried out with a loud voice, "My God, my God, why have you forsaken me?" (Matthew 27:46)
- who cried out again with a loud voice and breathed his last (Matthew 27:50)

- at whose death the curtain of the temple
  was torn in two, the earth shook, and the
  rocks were split (Matthew 27:51)
- who was taken down from the cross and
  laid in noble Joseph's own new tomb
  (Matthew 27:59–60)

Closing Prayer:
Lord Jesus Christ,
in your agony and bitter death,
you surrendered your spirit to your Father
and descended among the imprisoned spirits
to enlighten and release them.
Continue, in your mercy,
to break open the gates of death and hell
and to bring us to the resurrection of the body
and life everlasting in the world to come,
where you live and reign with the Father,
in the unity of the Holy Spirit,
one God, for ever and ever.
~AMEN.

After the Sorrowful Mysteries:

Salve Regina

Hail, holy Queen, Mother of mercy,

~HAIL, OUR LIFE, OUR SWEETNESS, AND OUR
HOPE.

TO YOU WE CRY, THE CHILDREN OF EVE;

TO YOU WE SEND UP OUR SIGHS,

MOURNING AND WEEPING IN THIS LAND OF
EXILE.

TURN, THEN, MOST GRACIOUS ADVOCATE,

YOUR EYES OF MERCY TOWARD US;

LEAD US HOME AT LAST

AND SHOW US THE BLESSED FRUIT OF YOUR
WOMB, JESUS:

O CLEMENT, O LOVING, O SWEET VIRGIN
MARY.[42]

Pray for us, holy Mother of God,

~THAT WE MAY BECOME WORTHY

OF THE PROMISES OF CHRIST.

Let us pray:

Almighty and everlasting God,
by the overshadowing of the Holy Spirit,
you prepared the humble Virgin Mary
to be a fit companion for your Son
as he walked the bitter road to Golgotha.
As we revere her compassion and her tears,
may we be set free by her motherly prayers
both from the ills of our present existence
and from the death that has no end.
We ask this through Christ, our blessed
        Savior.
~Amen.

Blessing
May the glorious passion of our Lord Jesus
        Christ
† bring us to the joys of paradise.
~Amen.

The Glorious Mysteries

"The angel said to the women, 'Do not be afraid; I know that you are looking for Jesus who was crucified. He is not here; for he has been raised, as he said. Come, see the place where he lay'" (Matthew 28:5–6).

In his pastoral letter on the Rosary, Pope John Paul II wrote:

The contemplation of Christ's face cannot stop at the image of the Crucified one. He is the Risen One! The Rosary has always expressed this knowledge born of faith and invited the believer to pass beyond the darkness of the Passion in order to gaze upon Christ's glory in the Resurrection and Ascension. Contemplating the Risen One, Christians *rediscover the reasons for their own faith* (cf. 1 Corinthians 15:14) and relive the joy not only of those to whom Christ appeared—the Apostles, Mary Magdalene, and the disciples on the road to Emmaus—but also *the joy of Mary,* who must have had an equally intense experience of the new life of her glorified Son. In the Ascension, Christ was raised in glory to the right hand of the Father, while Mary herself would be raised to that same glory in the Assumption, enjoying beforehand, by a unique privilege, the destiny reserved for all the just at the resurrection of the dead. Crowned in glory—as she appears in the last glorious mystery—Mary shines forth as the Queen of the Angels and Saints, the anticipation and the supreme realization of the eschatological state of the Church.

At the center of this unfolding sequence of the glory of the Son and the Mother, the Rosary sets before us the third glorious mystery, Pentecost, which reveals the face of the Church as a family gathered with Mary, enlivened by the powerful outpouring of the Spirit and ready for the mission of evangelization. The contemplation of this scene, like that of the other glorious mysteries, ought to lead the faithful to an ever greater appreciation of their new life in Christ, lives in the heart of the Church, a life of which the scene of Pentecost itself is the great "icon." The glorious mysteries thus lead the faithful to greater hope for the eschatological goal towards which they journey as members of the pilgrim People of God in history. This can only impel them to bear courageous witness to that "good news" which gives meaning to their entire existence.[43]

Julian of Norwich not only concentrated and enlarged upon the passion of Jesus but also on the glory of his risen life.

Very merrily and gladly our Lord looked into his side, and he gazed and said this: See how I loved you; as if he said: My child, if you cannot look on my divinity, see here how I suffered my side to be opened, and my heart to be split in two and to send out blood and water, all that was in it; and this is delight to me, and I wish it to be so for you.

Our Lord showed this to me to make us glad and merry. And with the same joyful appearance he looked down on his right, and brought to mind where our Lady stood at the time of his Passion, and he said: Do you wish to see her? And I answered and said: Yes, good Lord, great thanks, if it be your will. . . . And Jesus, saying this, showed me a spiritual vision of her. Just as before I had seen her small and simple, now he showed her high and noble and glorious and more pleasing to him than all creatures. And so he wishes it to be known that all who take delight in him should take delight in her, and in the delight that he has in her and she in him.[44]

I

GOD RAISES CHRIST
FROM THE GRAVE

Key Text: I handed on to you as of first importance what I in turn had received: that Christ died for our sins in accordance with the scriptures, and that he was buried, and that he was raised on the third day in accordance with the scriptures, and that he appeared to Cephas [Peter], then to the twelve. Then he appeared to more than five hundred brothers and sisters at one time, most of whom are still alive, though some have died. Then he appeared to James, then to all the apostles. Last of all, as to one untimely born, he appeared also to me (1 Corinthians 15:3–8).

Other Readings: Mark 16:1–8; Matthew 28:1–10; Luke 11:29–32; 24:1–11; John 20:1–10; Romans 6:1–14

Single Clause for Ten Hail Marys: who had to suffer and then enter into his glory (Luke 24:26)

Ten Clauses for Ten Hail Marys:
- who was in the heart of the earth for three days and three nights, alleluia! (Matthew 12:40)
- who was raised on the third day in accordance with the Scriptures, alleluia! (1 Corinthians 15:4)
- whom God raised from the dead, the first fruits of those who have died, alleluia! (1 Corinthians 15:20)
- who, being raised from the dead, will never die again, alleluia! (Romans 6:9)
- who descended among the dead to deliver them, alleluia! (1 Peter 3:19–20; 4:6)

- who overcame the sting of death and
  opened the kingdom of heaven to all
  believers, alleluia! (Te Deum)
- whom God has made both Lord and
  Messiah, alleluia! (Acts 2:36)
- whom God raised up and enthroned in the
  heavenly places, alleluia! (Ephesians 2:6)
- who is alive for ever and ever and holds
  the keys of Death and of Hades, alleluia!
  (Revelation 1:18)
- who makes all things new, alleluia!
  (Revelation 21:5)

Closing Prayer after the Gloria Patri
God of peace,
you sealed an eternal covenant
in the precious blood of Jesus
when you brought him back from the dead
to be the great Shepherd of your flock,
the one, holy, catholic, and apostolic Church.
By the holy waters of our baptism
and our anointing with chrism,

prepare us for a life of loving service
to our fellow human beings,
ready to do your will in all things.
We ask this through Jesus the Messiah,
to whom be honor and glory, now and for ever.
~AMEN.

Ten Alternate Clauses for the First Glorious Mystery:

- who had to suffer and then enter into his glory, alleluia! (Luke 24:26)
- about whom everything in the law of Moses, the prophets, and the psalms had to be fulfilled, alleluia! (Luke 24:44)
- who appeared first to Mary Magdalen in the garden of the tomb, alleluia! (John 20:1, 11–18)
- whose messengers appeared to the women who had followed Jesus from Galilee, alleluia! (Luke 24:1–10)
- who said to Mary Magdalen, "I am ascending to my Father and your Father

and to my God and your God," alleluia!
(John 20:17)

- who made himself known at Emmaus
  in the breaking of bread, alleluia! (Luke
  24:30–31)
- who came and stood among his disciples
  and showed them his hands and his side,
  alleluia! (John 20:20)
- who ate broiled fish in the presence of his
  disciples, alleluia! (Luke 24:42–43)
- who gave bread and fish to his disciples
  who were back fishing in the Lake of
  Galilee, alleluia! (John 21:13)
- who commanded his friends to make
  disciples of all nations, alleluia!
  (Matthew 28:19)

Closing Prayer after the Gloria Patri
Lord Jesus Christ,
as angels choirs rejoiced,
you rose from the dead on the third day,
mastering death by your death,
and canceling the power of sin.

By these mighty deeds on our behalf,
rescue us from our blindness and tepidity,
inspire us anew by your Holy Spirit,
and conduct us into a life of prayer and service
worthy of your awesome sacrifice,
O Savior of the world,
living and reigning with the Father and the
        Holy Spirit,
now and for ever.
~Amen.

2

JESUS ASCENDS INTO HEAVEN

Key Text: In the first book, Theophilus, I wrote about all that Jesus did and taught from the beginning until the day when he was taken up to heaven, after giving instructions through the Holy Spirit to the apostles whom he had chosen. After his suffering he presented himself alive to them by many convincing proofs, appearing to them during forty days and speaking about the kingdom of God. While staying with them, he ordered them not to leave Jerusalem, but to wait there for the promise of the Father. "This," he said, "is what you have heard from me; for John baptized with water, but you will be baptized with the Holy Spirit not many days from now.

You will receive power when the Holy Spirit has come upon you; and you will be my witnesses in Jerusalem, in all Judea and Samaria, and to the ends of the earth." When he had said this, as they were watching, he was lifted up, and a cloud took him out of their sight.

Then they returned to Jerusalem from the mount called Olivet, which is near Jerusalem, a sabbath day's journey away (Acts 1:1–5, 8–12).

Other Readings: Matthew 28:16–20; Mark 16:19–20; Luke 24:44–53; Ephesians 2:4–7

Single Clause: who sits at the right hand of God, with angels, authorities, and powers subject to him, alleluia! (1 Peter 3:22)

Ten Clauses for Ten Hail Marys:
• who is now crowned with glory and honor because of his suffering of death, alleluia! (Hebrews 2:9)

- who was taken up into heaven and seated at the right hand of God, alleluia! (Mark 16:19)

- who was exalted by God and given the name that is above every name, alleluia! (Philippians 2:9)

- who intercedes for us before the throne of God, alleluia! (Romans 8:34)

- who shines on those who dwell in darkness and the shadow of death, alleluia! (Luke 1:79)

- who called us out of darkness into his marvelous light, alleluia! (1 Peter 2:9)

- who made us a chosen race, a royal priesthood, a holy nation, God's own people, alleluia! (1 Peter 2:9)

- who sent out his apostles to make disciples of all nations, alleluia! (Matthew 28:19)

- who promised us the gift of the Holy Spirit, alleluia! (Luke 24:49; Acts 1:4)

- who will come again in glory to judge the living and the dead, alleluia! (Nicene Creed)

Closing Prayer after the Gloria Patri
Lord Jesus Christ, King of glory,
seated at the right hand of the Father,
do not leave us orphans
but send us the Promised of the Father,
the Spirit of truth,
who will fill us with all joy and consolation.
Blessed be the holy and undivided Trinity,
now and for ever.
~Amen.

3
PENTECOST: THE GIFT OF THE HOLY SPIRIT

Key Text: When the day of Pentecost had come, they were all together in one place. And suddenly from heaven there came a sound like the rush of a violent wind, and it filled the entire house where they were sitting. Divided tongues, as of fire, appeared among them, and a tongue rested on each of them. All of them were filled with the Holy Spirit and began to speak in other languages, as the Spirit gave them ability.

Now there were devout Jews from every nation under heaven living in Jerusalem. And at this sound the crowd gathered and was bewildered, because each one heard them speaking in the native language of each. Amazed and astonished, they asked, "Are not all these who are speaking Galileans? And how is it that we hear, each of us, in our own native language? In our own languages we hear them speaking about God's deeds of power." All were amazed and perplexed, saying to one another, "What does this mean?" But others sneered and said, "They are filled with new wine" (Acts 2:1–8, 11–13).

Other Readings: Genesis 11:1–9; Exodus 19:3–25; 20:1–21; Romans 8:1–27; John 7:37–39; John 14:15–21; Acts 4:23–31; Acts 10:44–48

Single Clause: who poured out his Spirit on the church (Acts 2:1–4)

Ten Clauses for Ten Hail Marys:
• who ransomed us with his own precious blood, alleluia! (1 Peter 1:19)

- who promised to stay with us to the end of the age, alleluia! (Matthew 28:20)
- who would not leave us orphans, alleluia! (John 14:18)
- whose Spirit rested on you, Mary, and on all his disciples, alleluia! (Acts 2:4)
- whose apostles went out and proclaimed the Good News everywhere, alleluia! (Acts 2:11)
- who pours out his Spirit on all the nations, alleluia! (Acts 10:45)
- whose Spirit has us speak the word of God with boldness, alleluia! (Acts 4:31)
- who clothes us with power from on high, alleluia! (Luke 24:49)
- who gives us another Advocate, the Spirit of truth, alleluia! (John 14:16–17)
- who sends forth his Spirit and renews the face of the earth, alleluia! (Psalm 104:30)

Closing Prayer after the Gloria Patri
Lord our God,
you desired that the Mother of your Son

should be present and joined in prayer
with the first Christian community.
Grant us the grace
to persevere with her in awaiting the Spirit,
that we may be one in heart and mind
and come to taste
the sweet and enduring fruits of redemption.
We ask this through our Lord Jesus Christ,
        your Son,
who lives and reigns with you and the Holy
        Spirit,
one God, for ever and ever.
~AMEN.[45]

4

MARY FALLS ASLEEP IN DEATH AND IS ASSUMED BODY AND SOUL INTO HEAVEN

Key Text: Listen, I will tell you a mystery! We will not all die, but we will all be changed, in a moment, in the twinkling of an eye, at the last trumpet. For the trumpet will sound, and the dead will be raised imperishable, and we will be changed. For this perishable body must put on imperishability, and this mortal body must put on immortality. When this perishable body puts on imperishability, and this mortal body puts on immortality, then the saying that is written will be fulfilled:

"Death has been swallowed up in victory."

"Where, O death, is your victory?

Where, O death, is your sting?"

The sting of death is sin, and the power of sin is the law. But thanks be to God, who gives us the victory through our Lord Jesus Christ (1 Corinthians 15:51–57).

Other Readings: 1 Chronicles 15:3–4, 16; 16:1–2; Judith 13:18–20; 15:9; John 11:17–27; 1 Corinthians 15:12–57; Revelations 21:1–6

Single Clause: who raised you body and soul to glory, alleluia!

Ten Clauses for Ten Hail Marys:
- who could not leave your soul among the dead nor let your holy body know decay, alleluia! (Psalm 16:10; Acts 2:27)
- who delivered you out of death, alleluia!
- who opened the gates of paradise for you, alleluia!
- who raised you body and soul to glory, alleluia!
- who exalted you above the choirs of angels, alleluia!

- who raised you imperishable and immortal, alleluia!
- who made you fair as the moon, bright as the sun, awesome as an army set in battle array, alleluia! (Song of Solomon 6:10)
- who made you more worthy of honor than the cherubim, and far more glorious than the seraphim, alleluia! (Byzantine Liturgy)
- who made you the glory of Jerusalem, the boast of Israel, the pride of our nation, alleluia! (Judith 15:9)
- who established you as the Mother of all the living, alleluia!

Closing Prayer after the Gloria Patri
Father in heaven,
all creation rightly gives you praise
for all life and holiness come from you.
In the plan of your wisdom
she who bore Christ in her womb
was raised body and soul to glory
to be with him in heaven.

May we follow her example in reflecting your
    holiness
and join with her hymn of endless life and
    praise.
We ask this through Christ our Lord.
~Amen.[46]

5

THE CORONATION OF MARY OUR QUEEN AND THE GLORY OF ALL THE SAINTS

Key Text: "I came forth from the mouth of the Most High, and covered the earth like a mist. I dwelt in the highest heavens, and my throne was in a pillar of cloud. Alone I compassed the vault of heaven and traversed the depths of the abyss. Over waves of the sea, over all the earth, and over every people and nation I have held sway. Among all these I sought a resting place; in whose territory should I abide? In the beloved city he gave me a resting place, and in Jerusalem was my domain. I took root in an honored people, in the portion of the Lord, his heritage" (Sirach 24:3–7, 11–12).

Other Readings: Matthew 5:1–16; Revelation 7:1–4, 9–12; Revelation 12:1–2; Revelation 21:1–4, 9–12

Single Clause: who set on your head a crown of twelve stars, alleluia! (Revelation 12:1)

Ten Clauses for Ten Hail Marys:
- who raised you above all women on earth, alleluia! (Judith 13:18)
- who created you altogether beautiful; there is no flaw in you, alleluia! (Song of Solomon 4:7)
- who made you more beautiful than the sun and every constellation of the stars, alleluia! (Wisdom 7:29)
- who set a crown of twelve stars on your head, alleluia! (Revelation 12:1)
- who clothed you with the sun and put the moon under your feet, alleluia! (Revelation 12:1)

- who made you like a rose of Sharon and
  a lily of the valley, alleluia! (Song of
  Solomon 2:1)
- who brought you up like a column
  of smoke, perfumed with myrrh
  and frankincense, alleluia! (Song of
  Solomon 3:6)
- who made you as comely as Jerusalem and
  as terrible as an army with banners, alleluia!
  (Song of Solomon 6:4)
- who declared you queen of all the saints in
  glory, alleluia!
- who willed that you be praised in every
  generation, alleluia! (Luke 1:48)

Closing Prayer after the Gloria Patri
Almighty God,
you gave a humble virgin
the privilege of being the mother of your Son,
and crowned her with the glory of heaven.
May the prayers of the Virgin Mary
bring us to the salvation of Christ

and raise us up to eternal life.
We ask this through our Lord Jesus Christ,
        your Son,
who lives and reigns with you and the Holy
        Spirit,
one God, for ever and ever.
~Amen.[47]

After the Glorious Mysteries: *Regina Coeli*
Rejoice, O Queen of heaven, alleluia!
~for the Son you bore, alleluia!
has arisen as he promised, alleluia!
Pray for us to God the Father,
        alleluia!

Rejoice and be glad, O Virgin Mary, alleluia!
~For the Lord has truly risen,
        alleluia!

Let us pray:

Loving Father,
by his life, death, and resurrection,

your dear Son won for us eternal bliss
at the heart of the Holy and Undivided
      Trinity.
By meditating on the mysteries of Mary's
      Rosary
may we imitate what they contain
and obtain what they promise,
through the same Christ our Lord.
~Amen.

By the power of Christ's dazzling resurrection
and of Mary's glorious assumption,
may God † conduct us to our heavenly home.
~Amen.

"The Rosary offers the 'secret' which leads us easily
to a profound and inward knowledge of Christ. We
might call it *Mary's way.* It is the way of the example
of the Virgin of Nazareth, a woman of faith, of
silence, of attentive listening. It is also the way of
Marian devotion inspired by the knowledge of the
inseparable bond between Christ and his Blessed
Mother: *the mysteries of Christ* are also in some

sense *the mysteries of his Mother,* even when they do not involve her directly, for she lives from him and through him."

Pope John Paul II,
Rosarium Virginis Mariae, # 24

The Litany of Loreto is often prayed at the conclusion of the Rosary.

Litany of Our Lady
(Loreto)

Lord, have mercy.	~LORD, HAVE MERCY.
Christ, have mercy.	~CHRIST, HAVE MERCY.
Lord, have mercy.	~LORD, HAVE MERCY.
God our Father in heaven,	~HAVE MERCY ON US.
God the Son,	
Redeemer of the world,	~HAVE MERCY ON US.
God the Holy Spirit,	~HAVE MERCY ON US.
Holy Trinity, one God,	~HAVE MERCY ON US.
Holy Mary,	~PRAY FOR US.
Holy Mother of God,	~PRAY FOR US.
Most honored of virgins,	~PRAY FOR US.
Mother of Christ,	~PRAY FOR US.
Mother of the Church,	~PRAY FOR US.
Mother of divine grace,	~PRAY FOR US.

Mother most pure,	~PRAY FOR US.
Mother of chaste love,	~PRAY FOR US.
Mother and virgin,	~PRAY FOR US.
Sinless Mother,	~PRAY FOR US.
Dearest of mothers,	~PRAY FOR US.
Model of motherhood,	~PRAY FOR US.
Mother of good counsel,	~PRAY FOR US.
Mother of our Creator,	~PRAY FOR US.
Mother of our Savior,	~PRAY FOR US.
Virgin most wise,	~PRAY FOR US.
Virgin rightly praised,	~PRAY FOR US.
Virgin rightly renowned,	~PRAY FOR US.
Virgin most powerful,	~PRAY FOR US.
Virgin gentle in mercy,	~PRAY FOR US.
Faithful virgin,	~PRAY FOR US.
Mirror of justice,	~PRAY FOR US.
Throne of wisdom,	~PRAY FOR US.
Cause of our joy,	~PRAY FOR US.
Shrine of the Spirit,	~PRAY FOR US.
Glory of Israel,	~PRAY FOR US.
Vessel of selfless devotion,	~PRAY FOR US.
Mystical rose,	~PRAY FOR US.
Tower of David,	~PRAY FOR US.
Tower of ivory,	~PRAY FOR US.
House of gold,	~PRAY FOR US.
Ark of the Covenant,	~PRAY FOR US.
Gate of heaven,	~PRAY FOR US.

Morning star,   ~PRAY FOR US.
Health of the sick,   ~PRAY FOR US.
Refuge of sinners,   ~PRAY FOR US.
Comfort of the troubled,   ~PRAY FOR US.
Help of Christians,   ~PRAY FOR US.

Queen of angels,   ~PRAY FOR US.
Queen of patriarchs and
    prophets,   ~PRAY FOR US.
Queen of apostles and martyrs,   ~PRAY FOR US.
Queen of confessors and virgins,   ~PRAY FOR US.
Queen of all saints,   ~PRAY FOR US.
Queen conceived in grace,   ~PRAY FOR US.
Queen raised up to glory,   ~PRAY FOR US.
Queen of the rosary,   ~PRAY FOR US.
Queen of families,   ~PRAY FOR US.
Queen of peace,   ~PRAY FOR US.

(Pause for spontaneous prayer.)

Lamb of God, you take away the sins of the world,
    ~HAVE MERCY ON US.
Lamb of God, you take away the sins of the world,
    ~HAVE MERCY ON US.
Lamb of God, you take away the sins of the world,
    ~HAVE MERCY ON US.

Pray for us, holy Mother of God,

~THAT WE MAY BECOME WORTHY OF THE PROMISES
OF CHRIST.

Let us pray:

Eternal God,
let your people enjoy constant health in mind and body.
Through the intercession of the Virgin Mary
free us from the sorrows of this life
and lead us to happiness in the life to come.
Grant this through Christ our Lord.
~AMEN.[48]

Appendix 1:
Other Marian Hymns
and Prayers

Te Matrem Laudamus

We praise you as our Mother,
   we acclaim you as our blessed Lady.
All the earth reveres you,
   the eternal Father's daughter.

The hosts of heaven and all the angelic powers
   sing your praise:
   the angels join in the dance,

the archangels applaud, the virtues give praise,
the principalities rejoice, the powers exult,
the dominations delight, the thrones make
    festival,
the cherubim and seraphim cry out unceasingly:

Holy, holy, holy is the great Mother of God,
    Mary most holy;
Jesus, the blessed fruit of your womb,
    is the glory of heaven and earth.

The glorious choir of apostles,
    the noble company of prophets,
    the white-robed army of martyrs,
    all sing your praise.

The holy Church throughout the world celebrates
        you:
    the daughter of infinite Majesty,
    the mother of God's true and only Son,
    the bride of the Spirit of truth and consolation.

You bore Christ, the King of glory,
    the eternal Son of the Father.
When he took our nature to set us free,
    he did not spurn your virgin womb.

When he overcame death's sting,
    he assumed you into heaven.
You now sit with your Son
    at God's right hand in glory.

Intercede for us, O Virgin Mary,
    when he comes to be our judge.
Help your chosen people,
    bought with his precious blood.
And bring us with all the saints
    into glory everlasting.

Save your people, holy Virgin,
    and bless your inheritance.
Rule them and uphold them,
    now and for ever.

Day by day we salute you;
    we acclaim you unceasingly.
In your goodness pray for us sinners;
    have mercy on us poor sinners.

May your mercy sustain us always,
    for we put our trust in you.
In you, dear Mother, do we trust;
    defend us now and for ever.[49]

Obsecro Te

Holy, glorious, and blessed Virgin Mary,
with great affection I address you,
daughter of the Most High,
mother of God's only Son,
and bride of the Holy Spirit.
You are more worthy of honor than the many-eyed
    cherubim
and far more glorious than the six-winged seraphim
who sing the hymn of victory to our Triune God.

Fountain of mercy and consolation,
source of piety and every joy,
be the mother of orphans,
the comforter of the afflicted,
a path for those who have gone astray,
and a refuge for all who put their hope in you.

By that holy gladness
when, at the message of the angel Gabriel,
you conceived the Son of God in your womb:

By that gracious acceptance and humility
by which you replied to Gabriel:
"Here am I, the servant of the Lord;
let it be with me according to your word."

By the overshadowing of the Holy Spirit,
who accomplished in you
the divine mystery of the Word made flesh:

By the mystic joy you experienced
when you brought forth your firstborn Son

in Bethlehem of Judea, the city of David,
and saw him acknowledged as Messiah and Lord.

By the overwhelming joy you felt
when you presented your newborn Son
to the awestricken shepherds of Bethlehem,
and the adoring wise men from the East
with their mystic gifts of gold, frankincense, and
      myrrh:

By those great and holy joys you experienced
when you and Joseph brought Jesus to the Temple
and the aged Simeon, filled with the Holy Spirit,
proclaimed him as a light of revelation to the
      nations
and the glory of his people Israel:

By the fear and desolation you underwent
when the tyrant Herod drove you into exile in Egypt
and murdered the holy innocents of Bethlehem
in his jealous and envious rage:

By your contemplative experience
of the quiet years in Nazareth of Galilee,
in the daily company of the Son of the Most High,
as he grew in wisdom and years,
and in divine and human favor:

By the profound experience of loss and separation
you experienced when your dear Son parted from
       you
to undergo his baptism by John in the Jordan,
and to begin his public ministry in Galilee:

By the sharp grief and deep compassion
you experienced when you saw your Jesus
stumbling along the way of the cross,
raised and hanging on the cross of pain,
and crying out to his Father as he died:

By the infinite pain you felt when a Roman spear
pierced the broken heart of the Man of Sorrows
and blood and water poured forth:

By the sword of sorrow that pierced your heart
as Joseph of Arimathea removed his body from the
        cross,
wrapped it in a linen shroud, and laid it in his own
        new tomb:

By your unshaken faith in your dead Jesus
as you cherished the promises and prophecies
of his rising on the third day:

By your keen joy in his dazzling resurrection
that vanquished death and hell,
brought life to those in the grave,
and made all things new:

By your delighted experience of his risen life
and the many convincing proofs he offered
to his chosen friends during forty days:

By his wonderful ascension into heaven
as he took his place at the right hand of the Father,
where he reigns in glory, now and for ever:

By your radiant encounter with the Holy Spirit of
        Pentecost
that clothed the apostles with power from on high
and empowered them to preach the Good News
throughout the whole world:

By your glorious assumption into heaven,
and your coronation as queen of all the saints in
        glory:

Gracious Lady of Mercy,
please come with all God's shining saints
to assist and support me in my every need.

Stand by me in each hour and moment of my life
and obtain for me from your beloved Son Jesus
every blessing and growth in holiness,
all peace and prosperity, all joy and gladness.

In the company of all the saints and angels,
watch over my immortal soul,
rule and protect my mortal body,
suggest holy thoughts to me,

beg pardon for my sins of the past,
help me amend my present life,
and prepare me for what is to come.

Above all, pray that I may entrust myself entirely
to the Good News proclaimed by your Son,
hope in his sure and loving promises,
and have sincere love for my neighbor.
Help me to lead an honorable and Christian life,
shield me from any form of mortal sin,
and defend me by your maternal prayers,
at the hour of my death.

By your unwearied intercession, O Mary,
may God graciously hear and receive this prayer
and bring me, by the merits of Christ my Savior,
to everlasting life in our heavenly home. Amen.[50]

Appendix 2:
Prayers and Litany
for a Wake

These prayers may be used to conclude any of the
Sorrowful and Glorious Mysteries used at a wake.

Lord Jesus Christ, King of glory,
deliver the souls of the faithful departed
from all the pains of death and hell.
May Michael the Archangel lead them into the
      holy light
that you promised to Abraham and Sarah
and their descendants in the faith.

May they come to enjoy a place
    of refreshment, light, and peace
with Mary, the Mother of God
and all the saints and angels,
and be one with you and your holy Father
and the life-giving Spirit,
now and for ever.
~AMEN.

Absolve, O Lord,
the souls of the faithful departed
from every bond of sin.
By the blood of Christ shed on the Cross,
enable them to escape the last judgment
and enjoy the happiness of eternal life
by the merits of the same Christ our Savior.
~AMEN.

Father of Jesus,
by the merits of Jesus our blessed Savior
you pardon all our sins
and lead us into heavenly bliss.
Please grant your servant, *Name,*

everlasting rest and the fellowship of all your saints.
We ask this through Christ our Lord.
~AMEN.

Loving Father in heaven,
by the intercession of the great Mother of God,
Mary most holy, and of all the saints,
please welcome the soul of our departed
  brother/sister
Name, into your holy presence.
May Christ be *his/her* Savior
and may the angels run to greet *him/her*
and conduct *him/her* into our heavenly home.
In Jesus' name we ask it.
~AMEN.

Creator and Redeemer of all those who believe in
  you,
grant the souls of your sons and daughters
the forgiveness of their sins
and the gift of life eternal with all your saints.
We ask this through Christ our Lord.
~AMEN.[51]

Merciful Father,

hear our prayers and console us.

As we renew our faith in your Son,

whom you raised from the dead,

strengthen our hope that all our departed brothers
    and sisters

will share in his resurrection,

who lives and reigns with you and the Holy Spirit,

one God, for ever and ever.

~AMEN.[52]

Lord God,

you are the glory of believers

and the life of the just.

Your Son redeemed us

by dying and rising to life again.

Since our departed brothers and sisters

believed in the mystery of your resurrection,

let them share the joys and blessings
    of the life to come.

We ask this through our Lord Jesus Christ your
        Son,

who lives and reigns with you and the Holy Spirit,

one God, for ever and ever.
~AMEN.[53]

God, our creator and redeemer,
by your power Christ conquered death
and returned to you in glory.
May all your people who have gone
    before us in faith
share his victory
and enjoy the vision of your glory for ever.
We ask this through our Lord Jesus Christ your
        Son,
who lives and reigns with you and the Holy Spirit,
one God, for ever and ever.
~AMEN.[54]

Litany of the Faithful Departed

At a wake service or anniversary of our beloved
dead, this litany may be used to complete the recitation of the Rosary.

Let us remember before God
all our departed brothers and sisters in Christ
who hope to share in his glorious Resurrection:

Lord, have mercy.	~LORD, HAVE MERCY.
Christ, have mercy.	~CHRIST, HAVE MERCY.
Lord, have mercy.	~LORD, HAVE MERCY.

God our Father in heaven,	~HAVE MERCY ON US.
God the Son, Redeemer of the world,	~HAVE MERCY ON US.
God the Holy Spirit,	~HAVE MERCY ON US.
Holy Trinity, one God,	~HAVE MERCY ON US.

Holy Mary, help of Christians,	~PRAY FOR THEM.
Holy Mary, health of the sick,	~PRAY FOR THEM.
Holy Mary, hope of the dying,	~PRAY FOR THEM.
Holy Mary, mother of the Church,	~PRAY FOR THEM.

St. Joseph, comfort of the troubled,	~PRAY FOR THEM.
St. Joseph, hope of the sick,	~PRAY FOR THEM.
St. Joseph, patron of the dying,	~PRAY FOR THEM.
St. Joseph, protector of the universal Church,	~PRAY FOR THEM.

St. Michael the Archangel, conductor of souls,	~PRAY FOR THEM.

St. Abraham and Sarah, our
    ancestors in the faith,   ~PRAY FOR THEM.
St. John the Baptist, forerunner
    of Christ,   ~PRAY FOR THEM.
St. Peter and Paul, apostles and
    martyrs,   ~PRAY FOR THEM.
All you holy saints of God,   ~PRAY FOR THEM.

Son of God and Savior
    of the world,   ~GOOD LORD, DELIVER THEM.
From all sin and suffering,   ~GOOD LORD, DELIVER THEM.
From the rigor of your justice,   ~GOOD LORD, DELIVER THEM.
From the grasp of the devil,   ~GOOD LORD, DELIVER THEM.
From long enduring sorrow,   ~GOOD LORD, DELIVER THEM.
From the loss of your holy
    presence,   ~GOOD LORD, DELIVER THEM.

By the mystery of your
    holy incarnation,   ~GOOD LORD, DELIVER THEM.
By your sacred birth at
    Bethlehem,   ~GOOD LORD, DELIVER THEM.
By your holy Name,
    Jesus-Savior,   ~GOOD LORD, DELIVER THEM.
By your manifestation to the
    Gentiles,   ~GOOD LORD, DELIVER THEM.
By your baptism, fasting, and
    temptation in the
    wilderness,   ~GOOD LORD, DELIVER THEM.

By your preaching of the Good
  News of the Kingdom,   ~GOOD LORD, DELIVER THEM.
By your transfiguration on
  Mount Tabor,   ~GOOD LORD, DELIVER THEM.
By your miracles of healing,   ~GOOD LORD, DELIVER THEM.
By your raising of the dead,   ~GOOD LORD, DELIVER THEM.
By your precious gift of the
  Holy Eucharist,   ~GOOD LORD, DELIVER THEM.
By your agony in the garden
  of Gethsemane,   ~GOOD LORD, DELIVER THEM.
By your holy cross and bitter
  passion,   ~GOOD LORD, DELIVER THEM.
By your precious death and
  burial,   ~GOOD LORD, DELIVER THEM.
By your glorious resurrection
  and wonderful ascension,   ~GOOD LORD, DELIVER THEM.
By your gift of the Holy Spirit,
  our guide and comforter,   ~GOOD LORD, DELIVER THEM.
At the hour of death and on
  the day of judgment,   ~GOOD LORD, DELIVER THEM.

(Pause for spontaneous prayers of intercession.)

Eternal rest grant unto them, O Lord,
~And let light perpetual shine upon them.

Let us pray:

O God, our creator and redeemer,
by your power Christ conquered death
and rose in glory on the third day.
May all who have gone before us in faith
share his victory over death
and enjoy the beatific vision for ever.
We make our prayer through Jesus our Lord.
~AMEN.

Lord of the living and of the dead,
by the prayers of the Blessed Virgin Mary
and of all the saints,
may our friends, relatives, and benefactors,
who have preceded us in death,
be welcomed into your paradise
of light, peace, and joy.
In Jesus' name, we ask it.
~AMEN.

May the souls of the faithful departed
through the mercy of God
† rest in peace.
~AMEN.

Appendix 3:
The Golden Rosary

Introduction

Praised and blest be the name of our Lord Jesus
   Christ
and the name of the glorious Virgin Mary for ever
   and ever!

The Apostles' Creed

Lord, have mercy. Christ, have mercy. Lord, have
mercy.

The Lord's Prayer and ten Hail Marys for each
decade.

After the word Jesus *in each Hail Mary,*
the following phrases are added:

First Decade

- whom you conceived by the overshadowing of the Holy Spirit
- whom John the Baptist recognized while he was still in the womb of his mother
- to whom you gave birth in Bethlehem of Judea
- whom you wrapped in bands of cloth and laid in a manger
- whom the angels proclaimed to the shepherds
- whom the shepherds found lying in a manger
- who was called Jesus at his circumcision, eight days after his birth
- whom the Magi adored and honored with gold, frankincense, and myrrh
- whom you offered in the Temple to the heavenly Father
- with whom you fled into Egypt and later returned to Nazareth

Praised and blest be the name of our Lord Jesus Christ and the name of the glorious Virgin Mary for ever and ever!

Second Decade

- whom you and Joseph lost in the Temple and found again after three days
- who went down with you to Nazareth and was obedient to you and Joseph
- whom John the Baptist immersed in the Jordan and called the Lamb of God
- who overcame Satan after fasting for forty days and nights in the desert
- who proclaimed the reign of God in the power of the Spirit
- who healed every kind of sickness and disease and raised the dead to life
- whose feet Mary of Bethany anointed with costly perfume and dried with her hair
- who was transfigured on Mount Tabor in the presence of Peter, James, and John

- who raised Lazarus to life again after he had been dead four days
- who entered Jerusalem in triumph on Palm Sunday

Praised and blest be the name of our Lord Jesus Christ and the name of the glorious Virgin Mary for ever and ever!

Third Decade
- who humbly washed the feet of his disciples at the Last Supper
- who gave them the Holy Eucharist, the mystery of faith
- who prayed in agony in the garden of Gethsemane
- who was betrayed by Judas and deserted by his friends
- who was denied by Simon Peter and mocked, spat upon, and beaten in the house of Caiaphas
- who was led away in chains to the court of Pontius Pilate
- who was clothed in the dress of a fool by Herod

- who was flogged like a slave and crowned with thorns
- who was handed over to be crucified and carried his cross to Golgotha
- whose cross bore the inscription: "Jesus of Nazareth, King of the Jews"

Praised and blest be the name of our Lord Jesus Christ and the name of the glorious Virgin Mary for ever and ever!

Fourth Decade
- who was deprived of his clothing and nailed to the cross between two criminals
- who was derided, mocked, and taunted by those who passed by
- who asked the Father to forgive those who crucified him
- who promised Paradise to the repentant criminal
- who from the cross commended you, O Mary, to his beloved disciple
- who was given sour wine to drink as he agonized on the cross

- who on the cross commended his spirit to the Father
- who at three o'clock cried out with a loud voice, "My God, my God, why have you forsaken me?"
- who said, "It is finished," bowed his head, and died
- whose side was pierced by a Roman spear after his death

Praised and blest be the name of our Lord Jesus Christ and the name of the glorious Virgin Mary for ever and ever!

Fifth Decade
- at whose death the earth shook, rocks were split, and tombs were opened
- whose broken body was placed in your lap
- whose body was wrapped in a linen shroud and laid in a rock-hewn tomb
- who proclaimed the Good News even to the dead
- who on the third day rose from the dead and appeared again and again to his friends

- who on the fortieth day ascended to his Father in heaven
- who on Pentecost sent us the Holy Spirit of truth and consolation
- who assumed you, body and soul, into heaven
- who crowned you Queen of all saints
- who will come again in glory to judge the living and the dead, alleluia!

Praised and blest be the name of our Lord Jesus Christ and the name of the glorious Virgin Mary for ever and ever!

Prayer
Blessed Virgin and Mother Mary,
refuge of sinners and comforter
    of the afflicted!
In your maternal love,
hear the prayers of those
    who put their trust in you.
Stand by us all in our need
and by the sufferings you endured

at the foot of the cross,
commend us to your crucified Son
that by his precious blood
we may attain eternal life.
~AMEN.[55]

Notes

1. Quoted by Julie Leininger Pycior in "We are called to be Saints: Thomas Merton, Dorothy Day and Friendship House," *The Merton Annual* 13 (2000): 43.

2. *A Book of Prayers* (Washington, DC: ICEL, 1982), 26, 35.

3. Ronald Knox, *The Priestly Life* (New York: Sheed and Ward, 1958), 143.

4. St. Justin Martyr (ca. 100–ca. 165), "Dialogue with Trypho the Jew," in *The Writings of Justin Martyr,* ed. T. Falls (New York: Christian Heritage, 1948), 304–05.

5. St. Irenaeus of Lyons (ca. 125–ca. 202), "Against the Heresies," in J. Quasten, *Patrology* (Westminster, MD: Newman Press, 1951), 1:297–98.

6. Tertullian (ca. 160–ca. 225), "De Carne Christi," in Luigi Gambero, SM, *Mary and the Fathers of the Church* (San Franciso: Ignatius Press, 1999), 67.

7. St. Augustine of Hippo (354–430), *Homily 2 on the Annunciation,* translated by the author.

8. St. Proclus of Constantinople (d. 446), "Sermon 1, On Mary," in *Documents in Early Christian Thought,* trans. Maurice Wiles and Mark Santer (New York: Cambridge University Press, 1977), 62. Delivered in the cathedral of Hagia Sophia in 428.

9. St. John of Damascus (ca. 675–ca. 749), *An Exact Exposition of the Orthodox Faith,* trans. Frederic H. Chase, Jr. (New York: Fathers of the Church, 1958), 292–93.

10. St. Ephrem of Syria (d. 373), translated from the Syriac by Kathleen McVey in *Divine Inspiration* (New York: Oxford University Press, 1998), 21. A deacon of the Christian church in Asia Minor, Ephrem was also a brilliant theologian whose medium was poetry. His hymns, written in Syriac, burst with paradox and symbol. They were popular in his day and are still used in the liturgy of the Syrian Church.

11. St. Proclus of Constantinople in a homily preached in the Christmas season of 428 or 429, translated by Brian Daley, SJ, in *On the Dormition of Mary* (Crestwood, NJ: St. Vladimir's Seminary Press, 1998), 2.

12. St. John of Damascus (ca. 675–ca. 749), "On the Dormition of the Holy Mother of God," in *On the Dormition of Mary,* trans. Brian Daley, SJ (Crestwood, NY: St. Vladimir's Seminary Press, 1998), 218.

13. G. G. Meersseman, OP, *The Akathistos Hymn* (Fribourg, Switzerland: Fribourg University Press, 1958), 20. Another translation was made by Vincent McNabb, OP, *Ode in Honor of the Holy Immaculate Most Blessed and Glorious Lady Mother of God and Ever Virgin Mary* (Oxford: Blackfriars, 1947).

14. Translated by Lazarus Moore in St. John Maximovitch, *The Orthodox Veneration of Mary, the Birthgiver of God* (Platina, CA: St. Herman of Alaska, 1996), 71–82; slighty modernized by permission.

15. Translation by the Rev. Professor Potter of Dublin and published in Cardinal Moran's "Essays on the Early Irish Church" Dublin, 1864. Reprinted in Daphne D. C. Pochin Mould, *The Celtic Saints* (New York: The Macmillan Company, 1956), 153.

16. Alcuin of York, *Missa sanctae Mariae,* ed. Jean Deshusses, OSB, *Le Sacramentaire gregorien* II (Fribourg, Switzerland: Fribourg University Press, 1979), #1841–1844, 45; translated by the author.

17. Edmund Bishop, *The Origin of the Prymer* (London: Kegan Paul, Trench, Trübner & Co., 1897); Jose M. Canal, CMF, "El Oficio Parvo de la Virgen de 1000–1250," *Ephemerides Mariologicae* 15 (1965): 463–75.

18. Claire Donovan, *The de Brailes Hours: Shaping the Book of Hours in Thirteenth-Century Oxford* (Toronto: University of Toronto Press, 1991). This is "the very first book of hours" produced in England and a particularly fine example of the genre and of the position and prominence of the Marian office in the Books of Hours. See also Astrik L. Gabriel, O Praem, *Student Life in Ave Maria College, Medieval Paris: History and Chartulary* (Notre Dame, IN: University of Notre Dame Press, 1955), which describes an example for young boys in a kind of prep school for the University of Paris.

19. Herbert Thurston, SJ, *The Month,* in Frank J. Sheed, *The Mary Book* (New York: Sheed and Ward, 1950), 241.

20. Cf. Herbert Thurston, SJ, *Familiar Prayers, Their Origin and History* (Westminster, MD: The Newman Press,

1953), 69–71 and Frank J. Sheed, *The Mary Book* (New York: Sheed and Ward, 1950), 239–40; translated by the author.

21. See appendix 3 for a full Golden Rosary. See also Hans Urs von Balthasar, *The Threefold Garland* (San Francisco: Ignatius Press, 1982), 15–17. On the origin and current use of the clausulae in Germany and further references: Yves Gourdel, O.Cart., "Le culte de la Tres Sainte Vierge dans l'Ordre des Chartreux," in ed. Hubert du Manoir, SJ, *Maria: Etudes sur la Sainte Vierge,* (Paris: Beauchesne, 1952), 2:657–75.

22. The best study of these developments is by Anne Winston-Allen, *Stories of the Rose* (University Park, PA: The Pennsylvania University Press, 1997), 13–80.

23. For remarkable examples of Rosary scenes on altar pieces, especially those of Veit Stoss of Nuremberg (ca. 1510–1520), see Michael Baxandall, *The Limewood Sculptors of Renaissance Germany* (New Haven: Yale University Press, 1980), 210–11.

24. English Language Liturgical Consultation (ELLC).

25. ELLC.

26. Pope John Paul II, *The Private Prayers of John Paul II* (New York: Pocket Books, 2002), 7.

27. Pope John Paul II, *Rosarium Virginis Mariae* (October 16, 2002), # 42.

28. Pope John Paul II, *Rosarium Virginis Mariae* (October 16, 2002), # 20.

29. Cf. Thomas Merton, *Conjectures of a Guilty Bystander* (Garden City, NY: 1968), 211 and "Fourteenth Century English Mystics," in *Newsletter* 4 (1978): 2.

30. Julian of Norwich, *Showings,* trans. Edmund Colledge, OSA and James Walsh, SJ (New York: Paulist Press, 1978), 131.

31. January 1, alternative prayer, Roman Missal.

32. Text: *Alma Redemptoris Mater,* trans. James Quinn, SJ, *Praise for All Seasons* (Pittsburgh: Selah, 1994), 97.

33. Pope John Paul II, *Rosarium Virginis Mariae* (October 16, 2002), # 21.

34. Julian of Norwich, *Showings* (long text), trans. Edmund Colledge, OSA and James Walsh, SJ (New York: Paulist Press, 1978), 240–41.

35. Prayer, Baptism of the Lord, Roman Missal.

36. Alternative prayer, Corpus Christi, Roman Missal.

37. *A Book of Prayers* (Washington, DC: ICEL, 1982), 35.

38. *Book of Mary* (Washington, DC: BCL, 1987), 5–6.

39. Pope John Paul II, *Rosarium Virginis Mariae*, (October 16, 2002), # 22.

40. Julian of Norwich, *Showings*, trans. Edmund Colledge, OSA and James Walsh, SJ (New York: Paulist Press, 1978), 125–26, 220–21.

41. English Prymer, ca. 1425, translated by the author.

42. *A Book of Prayers* (Washington, DC: ICEL, 1982), 34.

43. Pope John Paul II, *Rosarium Virginis Mariae*, (October 16, 2002), # 23.

44. Julian of Norwich, *Showings*, 146–47.

45. *Book of Mary* (Washington, DC: USCC, 1987), 8.

46. Alternative prayer, Assumption, Roman Missal.

47. Prayer, Vigil Mass of the Assumption, Roman Missal.

48. *Book of Prayers* (Washington, DC: ICEL, 1982), 28–29. A Marian litany containing some of these invocations was in use in the twelfth century. It was recorded in its present form (apart from a few additions by recent popes) at the Marian shrine of Loreto (Italy) in 1558 and approved by Pope Sixtus V (1521–1590).

49. Translated by the author from several Latin texts of the twelfth and thirteenth centuries.

50. The *Obsecro Te* derives from a large number of late medieval Books of Hours in both Latin and Middle English. Translated and expanded by the author.

51. These five prayers are translated by the author from the Tridentine Missal.

52. All Souls I, November 2, Roman Missal.

53. All Souls II, November 2, Roman Missal.

54. All Souls III, November 2, Roman Missal.

55. Translated and slightly altered by the author from *St. Mathias Gebet and Pilgerbuch* (Trier: Abbey of St. Mathias, 1933), 179–83.

Acknowledgments for the Complete Rosary

Several excerpts are taken from the Apostolic Letter, *Rosarium Virginis Mariae* by Pope John Paul II. Rome: Vatican Press, October 16, 2002.

An excerpt from POPE JOHN PAUL II, *The Private Prayers of Pope John Paul II*. English translation Copyright © 2002 by Libreria Editrice Rogate. Repinted by permission of Atria Books, an imprint of Simon and Schuster Adult Publishing Group.

Three excerpts from Dame Julian of Norwich are taken from Julian of Norwich, *Showings,* from the Classics of Western Spirituality translated from the Middle English by Edmund Colledge, OSA, and James Walsh, SJ. © 1978. Paulist Press Inc., New York/Mahwah, NJ. Used with permission. www.paulistpress.com

A quotation from Thomas Merton in Julie Leininger Pycior, "We are called to be saints," *The Merton Annual* 13(2000) no. 43. Used by permission of the editor Victor A. Kramer, Catholic University Center, Emory University, 1753 N. Decatur Rd., Atlanta, GA 30007.

A quotation form Ronald Knox, *The Priestly Life.* © 1958, Sheed and Ward. By permission A P Watt Ltd on behalf of The Earl of Oxford and Asquith.

A quotation from Justin Martyr's *The Writings of Justin Martyr,* ed. T. Falls, © 1948, Heritage Press.

A quotation from Johannes Quasten, © 1951, Newman Press. Used with permission of Paulist Press. www.paulistpress.com

A quotation from Kathleen McVey, *Ephrem the Syrian,* from the Classics of Western Spirituality, © 1989, Paulist Press. Used with permission of Paulist Press. www.paulistpress.com

A quotation from Luigi Gambero, SM, *Mary and the Fathers of the Church.* © 1999, Ignatius Press. Permission granted by Ignatius Press, San Francisco.

A quotation from Maurice Wiles and Mark Santer, *Documents in Early Christian Thought.* © 1977, CUP. Reprinted with the permission of Cambridge University Press.

The first Kontakion and Eikos of the Akathist of Our Lady in The Orthodox Veneration of Mary by St. John Maximovitch, 6th printing, third edition, © 2004, pages 71–72; language slightly modernized by WGS with the specific permission of Fr. Damascene, the St. Herman of Alaska Brotherhood, P.O. Box 70, Platina, CA 96076-0070.

A quotation from G. G. Meerssemann, OP, *The Akathistos Hymn,* © 1958, Fribourg University Press.

A poem from Daphne D. C. Pochin Mould, *The Celtic Saints*. © 1956. Clonmore and Reynolds, Dublin, Ireland.

Two quotations from Frank Sheed, *The Mary Book*. © 1950, Sheed and Ward. Copyright administered by the Continuum International Publishing Group Ltd.

Three quotations from Brian Daley, SJ, *On the Dormition of Mary*. © 1998, St. Vladimir Seminary Press. By permission of St. Vladimir Seminary Press, 575 Scarsdale Rd., Crestwood, NY 10707. www.svs.com

A hymn "Mother of Christ, our Hope, our Patroness," from James Quinn, SJ. Used by permission of Selah Publishing Co., Inc. North American agent. www.selahpub.com. Used by permission. License no. pending.

About the Author

William G. Storey is professor emeritus of Liturgy and Church History at the University of Notre Dame. He has compiled, edited, and authored some of the best-loved prayer books of our time, most notably *Lord, Hear Our Prayer; Hail Mary: A Marian Book of Hours; An Everyday Book of Hours;* and *Mother of the Americas.* He resides in South Bend, Indiana.